S0-AFW-648

THE MELTDOWN YEARS

THE MELTDOWN YEARS

YEARS

THE UNFOLDING OF THE GLOBAL ECONOMIC CRISIS

WOLFGANG MÜNCHAU

New York Chicago San Francisco Lisbon London
Madrid Mexico City Milan New Delhi San Juan
Seoul Singapore Sydney Toronto

The *McGraw·Hill* Companies

Copyright © 2010 by Carl Hanser Verlag München. All rights reserved.
Printed in the United States of America. Except as permitted under the United
States Copyright Act of 1976, no part of this publication may be reproduced or
distributed in any form or by any means, or stored in a data base or retrieval
system, without prior written permission of the publisher.

1 2 3 4 5 6 7 8 9 0   DOC/DOC   0 1 0 9

ISBN: 978–0–07–163478–6

MHID: 0–07–163478–9

This publication is designed to provide accurate and authoritative information
in regard to the subject matter covered. It is sold with the understanding that
the publisher is not engaged in rendering legal, accounting, or other
professional service. If legal advice or other expert assistance is required, the
services of a competent professional person should be sought.

*—From a Declaration of Principles Jointly Adopted by a Committee of the American
Bar Association and a Committee of Publishers and Associations*

McGraw-Hill books are available at special quantity discounts to use as
premiums and sales promotions, or for use in corporate training programs. To
contact a representative, please visit the Contact Us pages at
www.mhprofessional.com.

This book is printed on acid-free paper.

CONTENTS

PROLOGUE

*M*eltdown Years is the story of our Great Crisis. But it is a story of a different kind. We are not obsessing with the trivia of this crisis, how devious mortgage salespeople defrauded an innocent American public, how hedge funds and rating agencies conspired to corrupt the world, or how Alan Greenspan or George W. Bush got it all wrong. Apportioning blame for this crisis may be fun, but it is a dead-end road for anyone who seeks an understanding of what happened. Our crisis is a story of human failure, for sure, but it is first of all a story of systems failure. If you want to believe that this was a case of bad people wrecking an otherwise good system, you should perhaps read another book.

We are also not blaming America or American capitalism. There is no question that the specific problems in the credit markets originated in the United States, but, just like the Great Depression, this is not a story that can be fully or even adequately understood in the context of America alone. Unlike many other books on this subject, *Meltdown Years* takes a global perspective.

This is a contentious proposition. Former President Bill Clinton, when asked who is to blame for the crisis, answered without hesitation: America. I believe the correct answer is more complex, and more disturbing. Many eminent economists agree with Clinton, among them Martin Feldstein, an economic advisor to President Ronald Reagan, and a long-time president of the National Bureau of Economic Research. Feldstein gave six reasons for this crisis—mostly American reasons: U.S. interest rates had been too low; financial regulation had been insufficiently focused; bad housing policies had set wrong incentives; rating agencies had misled investors; the banking system had failed to account for risk properly; and borrowers had taken on too much debt. Feldstein's six reasons would indeed place most, if not all, of the blame on U.S. policy, U.S. institutions, and individual Americans. But his analysis is superficial. We should ask ourselves: Why has there been regulatory failure, why did people take on so much debt, and why did the Federal Reserve (the Fed) cut interest rates to such extremely low levels, as it did during 2003 and 2004? These are the questions one needs to answer to fully understand how this crisis has arisen. In the search for answers, one invariably encounters the global economy, the global monetary system, and the global financial system.

Meltdown Years takes the reader on a journey starting in the early 1970s and ends in 2009, in the hope of presenting a broader picture of our crisis. It is written for people who have a serious interest in the subject, but who are not financial market experts. In that sense, *Meltdown Years* is also a primer that aims to furnish the reader with sufficient background knowledge to understand what happened, and to follow the present debate about the economic recovery, how to rescue the banking sector, and what consequences to draw for the future of financial capitalism.

To this effect, *Meltdown Years* contains several sidebars, written specifically for the nonexpert, to explain some fundamental concepts in greater detail, for example: How does a bank balance sheet work, or what is a swap? There is no point in talking about generalities, such as "toxic assets," or using even stranger metaphors as newspapers often do. We need to dig a bit deeper, in search for greater precision, to understand how the credit scam actually worked.

Likewise, it would be oversimplified simply to state the obvious fact that the United States has been living beyond its means, without an understanding of the complex global interactions that produced its consumer credit craze in the first place. For this reason we need to take a closer look at the way the global economy has contributed to this crisis. If you are an expert, or in a hurry, you can omit the sidebars without losing the plot of our narrative. They are strictly optional, but they will be of great help to the novice.

I started with the first version of this book in February 2007, when the global meltdown was not a meltdown yet but a bubble. The purpose at the time was to warn about a dangerous bubble that might burst within a few years. The first two editions were written for the German market, my home country, a country in which many people understand the functioning of a motor car or a turbine, but have a very rudimentary knowledge of modern finance. For that reason I took the approach to explain the danger, and later the crisis, in some detail, assuming the readers had absolutely no knowledge even about the existence of a credit market, let alone about what MBS, CDO, and CDS stand for. As it turned out, even bankers, financial journalists, and economists who did not specialize in finance, told me that they found the book useful as a primer for the crisis. *Meltdown Years* started off as a project of explanation, in narrative form, and it still retains that approach in the much updated and much improved U.S. edition.

I have also included a glossary at the end of the book that provides short definitions of the main terms used in this book. Use it whenever you come across a term you are not familiar with or one the meaning of which you have forgotten. There is an Appendix to give a short history of financial crises. Financial crises are all different, but they are all similar too. I describe some parallels with earlier crises.

As an economic columnist for the London-based *Financial Times*, I have written *Meltdown Years* as an unashamedly journalistic book using the definition of journalism as a first draft of history. I certainly do not pretend to have produced a history of the crisis or the definitive analysis—for which it is almost certainly too early in any case. Some of the best books on the Great Depression came out years, even decades after the event itself. As I am writing about this crisis from within this crisis, my angle of observation, as that of any other author who currently writes, is naturally distorted.

Meltdown Years is journalistic in another respect—in terms of its viewpoint, which I would characterize as that of the semi-neutral observer. I will not shove my favorite theory down the readers' throats, and I will try to do justice to other viewpoints which present alternative theories about the causes and the consequences of this crisis. There exists, as yet, no complete consensus about the crisis, only a series of competing explanations. I will not shy away from stating what I believe to be plausible, or not. In other words, I shall not pretend to be neutral when I am not. I shall seek to be fair, however, and leave it to the reader to decide whether I have succeeded in this endeavor. In particular, I will challenge the currently fashionable consensus view, according to which this crisis is first and foremost the result of regulatory failure in the United States. I believe it is at least as much a crisis of global economic policy. This is also one of the book's main conclusions.

While the two German editions of this book focused narrowly on the crisis itself, and its precise mechanisms, I am able to offer in this first U.S. edition a much broader historic sweep, and a deeper discussion about its causes and possible consequences. The intervening two years have not only brought up many facts and discussions, they have also given us time to think about some of these issues in greater depth. The final chapter of the book is solely devoted to that discussion. It offers my analysis of the events. Readers who are mainly interested in a detailed discussion of the causes of the crisis and the implications for policy could start directly with the last chapter.

The book is divided into three chapters. The first presents the history up until the bubble burst, starting with banking crises in the United Kingdom and Germany in the early 1970s, and the regulatory response. Knowledge of this history is absolutely critical for a deeper understanding of what happened later. The first chapter offers a narrative of the events leading directly up to the current crisis, the U.S. property boom, the credit boom in particular, the ultra-modern financial instruments, and how they were used to create and accentuate the bubble. The ambitious goal of this chapter is to explain, in gory detail, how the speculative bubble in the credit markets actually worked.

The second chapter is the story of the financial meltdown, how it got started, how it spread, and how it interacted with the real economy. What started as a financial crisis turned into an economic recession, and in some countries even into a full-fledged depression. At the time of writing during the spring of 2009, there was evidence that global trade had collapsed at a speed similar to, or even greater than, that during the Great Depression.

The third and final chapter presents the various competing explanations about the causes of the crisis, and concludes that the main cause is an inherently unstable global economic system. It also offers an outlook on how long the crisis might last, what policy options should be deployed, and the long-term consequences of the crisis for society on the whole.

The start of our narrative does not take place in the world of subprime lending in Florida but several thousand miles away from the crime scene, and several decades earlier, in the British city of London and in the German city of Cologne.

CHAPTER 1

BEFORE THE MELTDOWN

I n 2003, Robert Lucas, a Nobel Prize–winning economist teaching at the University of Chicago, claimed the "central problem of depression-prevention has been solved, for all practical purposes, and has in fact been solved for many decades." It was probably one of the biggest economic misjudgments of our time, but let there be no doubt: It was misjudgment, not stupidity, that gave rise to this error. It reminds us of a similar misjudgment by another great economist. In 1929, just days before the stock market crash, Irving Fisher almost destroyed his reputation when he said that "stock prices have reached what looks like a permanently high plateau."

We should remember that both of these statements seemed obviously true to many people on the day they were made. Many economists agreed with Lucas back in 2003, and they did so until the summer of 2008. Fisher merely said what many others were thinking at the time. But just as those statements appeared obviously true at the time, they suddenly appeared false, just as "obviously." Looking at it with hindsight, everything is so easy, so obvious. It is the eternal delusion of the hindsight observer.

People always try to rationalize the bubble, to explain why house prices would continue to rise, even after they had trebled in value, or why the Dow Jones Industrial Average would soon hit 36,000, as one unfortunate forecaster claimed. Nothing is more alienating than listening to what people used to say during those days, which is really not that long ago. But very few people at the time sounded the warning bells. Those who did were denounced as doom-mongers. Denouncing those doom-mongers was not even that difficult, because year after year they were proven wrong. This was the age of the optimist, the age of the gambler, who had no time for financial economics, of history, let alone doubt. It took a minimal understanding of history and economics to see this crisis coming.

The British have a saying: "The past is a foreign country. They do things differently over there." This is exactly how it feels when one looks at this not-too-distant past, if one listens to what people were saying then. And for that reason we need to delve into history, when some of the seeds of the present crisis were planted. Our first chapter starts in a foreign country—literally, that is.

When Banks Go Bust

Finance was pretty stable in the 1950s and 1960s. This was an age of extraordinary economic stability. Most exchange rates were tied to the dollar in a system known as Bretton Woods.

The name comes from the system's 1944 birthplace in New Hampshire.

The 1950s and 1960s were also a period of extraordinary financial stability. The world still benefited from the many changes in economic policy that resulted from the Great Depression. The gold standard that was still in place during the Depression was one of the great global amplifiers of economic shocks in the early 1930s. The new Bretton Woods was also a gold standard of sorts, but it was more flexible, as exchange rates were allowed to adjust from time to time. This was still an age in which banking and investment banking were separate, when financial innovation was slow, and regulation was tough. It appeared during those years that the world had solved the recurring problem of financial instability for good. Bank runs were considered a disease of the past, much like smallpox.

In the early 1970s, the illusion of eternal financial stability would end abruptly. One of the first modern crises took place in Great Britain, which had a large housing boom at the time—not as large as our recent one, but very large nevertheless. Banks had lent too much money to homeowners, as everybody believed that the house price boom of that period would last forever. Sound familiar? When house prices subsequently collapsed, the banks discovered that they had insufficient collateral. Some banks were technically insolvent. Banking was a lot simpler then than it is today. There was no subprime market, no securitization, none of the toolkits of modern finance. But other than that, the situation was not that fundamentally different: Hubris about house prices leads to excessive credit, which leads to more hubris. At one point this game collapses. Economists refer to this as a Ponzi game, named after Charles Ponzi, an American swindler who lived in the early part of the twentieth century, who duped his victims with a mind-boggling pyramid scheme. Much of modern banking is in the same spirit. And the ghost of Ponzi fell over the city of London in the early 1970s.

One of the biggest surprises one realizes when studying financial crises across countries and across decades—even centuries—is how similar they all are. Most financial crises involve excessive lending secured on assets with fast collapsing values. The British eventually resolved their first truly modern financial crisis through a bailout. The Bank of England, the central bank of the United Kingdom, rescued some 30 banks in the 1970s. Finance was not as big as it is today, and rescuing the banking sector was a smart thing to do. At the time, countries could actually afford it without getting into difficulty themselves. This is probably the main difference between the bailouts of 30 years ago and today.

The British central bank acted according to a doctrine created in the nineteenth century by Walter Bagehot, an editor of the *Economist* magazine, who said a central bank should never allow an important bank to go bust. It should always bail it out, but do so at a punitive price to avoid what economists call "moral hazard." It means: Do not create an incentive for others to misbehave as well, in the hope that they, too, will be bailed out. Bagehot's famous doctrine survived for a long time, but for the current crisis the doctrine is much more difficult to apply because the banking sector has become so big that countries are no longer in the position to bail out every bank. Belgium's largest bank, Fortis, had assets greater than the annual economic output of the entire country. In Iceland, the banking sector was almost nine times as large as the country's annual economic output. So banks that were regarded as too big to fail suddenly became too big to save. It would have been easier for Fortis to bail out Belgium, and for Iceland's banks to bail out Iceland, rather than the other way around.

But that was not the case in the United Kingdom back in the early 1970s. The crisis ended with a bailout, in the tradition of Bagehot. All was well.

There was no such happy ending for Herstatt Bank in Cologne, Germany, a city not known for its financial savvy, but for its magnificent cathedrals and its modern art markets. One morning in 1974, German bank regulators walked into the bank and closed it down after it had incurred serious losses in foreign exchange transactions. Bagehot's famous doctrine, to the extent that it was known in Germany, would not have applied here, since Herstatt was considered a relatively small and insignificant bank. This turned out to have been a big misjudgment. And as every reader knows today, it was not the last time that such a misjudgment would be made.

Herstatt was a private bank. Founded in the late eighteenth century, the Herstatt family sold the bank in the nineteenth century, and then bought it back again in 1955. It was a tiny local bank at the time that specialized in providing funding to small nonprofit societies, churches, newspapers, and even brothels—a rather unusual combination of customers. But something strange happened during this period. Between 1955 and 1973 this little neighborhood bank was able to raise its total assets from an equivalent of $1 million to almost $1 billion, an increase by a factor of 1,000!

One of the reasons for this miraculous transition was a rogue trader by the name of Dany Dattel, who was tremendously successful in his early days. Dattel was head of the bank's small foreign exchange operations, which suddenly became a lucrative business in the early 1970s when the Bretton Woods system of semi-fixed global exchange rates collapsed. The switch from fixed to floating exchange rates offered an ideal source of activity for speculators like Dattel. But not only professionals took part in this speculation. The German news magazine *Der Spiegel* reported the story that a secretary won a six-figure sum in a single foreign exchange bet, and that a young trainee builder was able to afford a Porsche car valued at several decades' worth of his annual earnings. Exuberance bred further exuberance, and ordinary people became active participants in the game.

In early 1974, the foreign exchange traders at Herstatt got it badly wrong. They speculated on a rising dollar, but the opposite happened, and they lost some 1.4 billion Deutsche Marks in the space of just four months. That sum exceeded the bank's capital to a large extent. The following day, the investors lined up outside, angrily demanding their money back, but the regulators had arrived there first.

It was the first notable bank failure of that time. But the reason it became so notorious was a different one. The bank had also engaged in so-called currency swap operations, which is normally a fairly riskless business. In this particular case, the bank exchanged dollars for Deutsche Marks (DM) at some agreed rate. But there is a time difference of six hours between Eastern Standard Time in New York and Central European Time in Cologne. At the moment, when the regulators walked in, Herstatt had already received the dollars from its U.S. counterparts, but had not yet paid the Deutsche Marks, which they could only have done after business started in New York several hours later. But by the time New York had opened, Herstatt had already been shut down, and was not able to complete its part of the transaction. Within the same time zone, that problem could not have arisen. The two payments would have been swapped instantaneously. The entire deal would either have gone through before the bank ceased operations, or it would have failed. It was only because of the time difference that Herstatt's U.S. counterparts did not get their money back.

The risk encountered by the U.S. banks is known as settlement risk, subsequently known as Herstatt risk. It could have produced a dangerous series of cascading bank collapses. If the losses by the U.S. banks had been sufficiently large, they could have been technically insolvent as well. The principal reason why banks are so vulnerable to a large loss in exchange rate speculation, as in the case of Herstatt, or the exposure to settlement risk, is the fact that banks have relatively little capital in relation to the enormous amounts of money they play with each day. Back at the time, there were no agreed international rules how much capital a bank should hold. The more capital, the more protected a bank is against shocks. Capital is the shock absorber for banks. If a bank makes a loss, for example, if loans do not get repaid, or if securities the bank owns suddenly fall in value, the loss comes out of the bank's capital. If the loss exceeds the capital, the bank is insolvent. But even if it does not, the bank can still be in trouble if the ratio of capital to assets falls below a minimum threshold.

The following discussion explains the basis of a bank balance sheet. It is probably the single most important technical concept in this book.

What Is a Bank?

You may think you know the answer to the question: What is a bank? However, you might be wrong. Surely you know that the core business of a classic bank is to accept money from investors at a specific interest rate and lend it to customers at a higher rate. That is trivially true, unfortunately we need to have a few more facts about banks to understand how banking crises can arise, and what happens to banks during this time.

It is important to have a rudimentary understanding of a bank's balance sheet. In the real world, a balance sheet has many more entries than the rather simplified version we are producing below. But this is all we need to understand how a bank gets into trouble. Shown here are the two sides of a bank's balance sheet—its assets and its liabilities:

Assets	Liabilities
Loans	Savings deposits and checking accounts
+ Securities held, valued at market prices	+ Borrowings from other banks, central bank
	+ Shareholders' capital
= Total Assets	= Total Liabilities

For those of you not familiar with balance sheets, the first rule of accounting is not to use common sense. That would be very confusing. You might think, for example, that having lots of capital is an asset for a bank, and you would actually be right. But a balance sheet takes a different viewpoint. An asset is something that a bank owns, or thinks it owns—for example, a security held in its trading portfolio. It is a claim on a third party. If a bank makes a loan, it has a claim on future repayments. All these loans and securities are grouped together in the bank's balance sheet under "assets."

The other side of the balance sheet includes the bank's liabilities. Liabilities are, loosely speaking, what the bank owes, or more precisely, claims that others have on the bank. A bank deposit, for example, counts as a liability, because a depositor can always walk in and claim the money back. Capital is also a liability, though this is perhaps not very straightforward. But capital represents a claim by the owners of the bank, the shareholders, in respect of future dividends. Capital is thus a liability for the bank, and an asset for the shareholders. The words in our day-to-day language often have different meanings than the words in their technical definitions. It is always best to think of assets as claims you have on others, and liabilities as claims others have against you.

The most important point to remember is that a balance sheet must balance at all times. So if the assets go up, because the stock market has risen, liabilities must go up as well, otherwise there would be no balance. Likewise, if the assets fall in their value, liabilities must also fall. So when assets change, what bit of the liabilities goes up or down? Our simplified balance sheet contains only three items on the liability side:

(Continued)

deposits, loans from the central bank and other banks, and capital. Since deposits and loans have not changed, a fall in the value of assets must come out of capital. And capital is owned by the shareholders. So if a bank's assets go down, the shareholders take a hit.

Let us illustrate this with an example.

Say a bank has $100 million in assets. Let's assume for the sake of simplicity, the bank has all its assets in the form of mortgages. It has lent the entire $100 million to homeowners. Let's assume further, that the bank has $95 million in checking accounts, and $5 million of capital, and no loans from other banks or the central bank. In reality, a bank's balance sheet will be more complicated. It will list different classes of assets and liabilities, but for the sake of this demonstration, this complication is irrelevant.

Following is the balance sheet for our Simplified Mortgage Bank:

Assets	$ (in millions)	Liabilities	$ (in millions)
Mortgage loans	100	Checking accounts	95
		Capital	5
Total Assets	**100**	**Total Liabilities**	**100**

With assets of $100 million and capital of $5 million, the bank has a leverage ratio of 20 (assets divided by capital). Now assume the bank suffers a loss on its mortgage loan portfolio—there is a property crash, and not all of its customers repay. Let us first assume that the loss is $3 million. What is the effect on the balance sheet?

Assets	$ (in millions)	Liabilities	$ (in millions)
Mortgage loans	97	Checking accounts	95
		Capital	2
Total Assets	**97**	**Total Liabilities**	**97**

The assets would no longer be valued at $100 million, but only at $97 million. But since a balance sheet has to balance, the liabilities must also fall by the same amount. The bank deposits do not change. People still have their accounts in the bank, and could claim their money back at any moment. So the only item in the balance sheet that has wiggle room is the capital. The capital gets reduced from $5 million to $2 million. So we now have a balance sheet showing $97 million in assets and liabilities, respectively. But the capital is now only $2 million, and the leverage ratio is now close to 50 (total assets divided by capital, or 97/2). At that point, the bank is in some danger. With only $2 million in capital, it tries to manage some $97 million in assets.

This is the moment when the red lights should start to flash. But what happens if the housing crisis gets worse, and the bank loses another $2 million?

Assets	$ (in millions)	Liabilities	$ (in millions)
Mortgage loans	95	Checking accounts	95
		Capital	0
Total Assets	**95**	**Total Liabilities**	**95**

Assets would fall from $97 million to $95 million. On the liability side, the customer deposits remain unchanged at

(Continued)

$95 million. For the balance sheet to balance the capital becomes zero. In other words, the shareholders are wiped out.

If there are even more losses, the capital would become negative. Since banks and other large companies are limited liability corporations, the shareholders actually don't owe any of the money. The most they stand to lose is what they have put in. So the shareholders are not necessarily bankrupt, but the bank almost certainly is.

This simple calculation has been known to economists and bank regulators forever. If you want a solid banking system, you must find some mechanism to enforce a sensible relationship between a bank's capital and its assets. If something goes wrong, as things do from time to time, you want the buffer to be big enough that a bank can withstand a fall in its assets without being wiped out.

When something goes wrong, it is very important to distinguish between a bank that is insolvent, and one that has no liquidity. In the case of Herstatt, the situation was evident. The bank lost more than it had. It was bankrupt, and this was immediately clear. But in our crisis, the situation was more opaque.

Insolvency is what happens when a bank's capital falls toward zero. Illiquidity means that a bank does not have the cash to pay out a depositor who closes the account, or to repay a loan, for example, from another bank. In the past, illiquidity occurred frequently as a result of bank runs, usually triggered by false rumors. There were many such occurrences in the United States during the nineteenth century when the banking systems were still rudimentary. Investors would seek to withdraw their money, only to find that their banks, which had already lent the money to borrowers, suddenly lacked sufficient liquidity to pay back the investors. The banks, unable to obtain liquidity quickly enough, were often forced to close their doors. Anyone who saw the movie *It's a Wonderful Life* knows exactly the importance of having enough cash in the till right up until the bank closes its door in the evening.

Back in the old days, after a bank run, a bank was often shut down, but the important thing to remember is that these banks were usually solvent. Their balance sheets were probably healthy in the sense that at any point in time there was sufficient capital in relationship to assets. There was much banks could do to protect themselves against insolvency—by maintaining an adequate ratio of capital to assets. But managing liquidity is more difficult. No bank in the world would be capable of surviving a bank run without external help.

Basle

In the early 1970s, there was no formal regulation that imposed limits on the banks' leverage on a truly global scale. After the Herstatt crisis, governments agreed that what was needed was a global solution to ensure that all banks that participated in worldwide transactions meet a minimum set of rules, to be enforced by domestic regulators. The Herstatt collapse gave rise to a long and arduous process, which resulted in a globally accepted system for capital adequacy regulations. In the aftermath of the Herstatt collapse, a group of regulators and central bankers met regularly in the Swiss city of Basle, home to the Bank for International Settlements (BIS), an august institution that has often been referred to as the central bank for central banks. The purpose of these meetings was to structure a globally acceptable banking system.

The BIS was one of the institutions founded near the end of the Great Depression to help prevent such calamities in the future. During the Bretton Woods regime of semi-fixed exchange rates from 1944 until the early 1970s, there were relatively few crises, and the BIS somewhat lost its sense of purpose. Many people began to question the usefulness of such an institution. The International Monetary Fund (IMF) and the World Bank dealt with sudden crises and development issues. The BIS was not a lender of last resort; to some it was little more than a central bankers' think tank.

But the Herstatt collapse gave the BIS a new lease on life. The meeting of regulators turned into a series of semipermanent political processes. The idea was to make the incipient process of financial globalization shockproof against the kind of risks that were evident in the Herstatt collapse. One of those risks was obviously the settlement risk, the Herstatt risk. But this was only a relatively minor technical issue that was resolved relatively quickly. It plays no part in our narrative. The real issue was capital adequacy—ensuring that a bank had enough capital to withstand a serious shock.

It was a long and arduous process. The Basle Committee prepared a set of rules that were later known as "Basle I." These rules gave a very clear and strict definition of how much capital a bank needs. The basic rule is that capital has to be a minimum of 8 percent of risk-weighted assets. "Risk-weighted" means that certain assets, like a business loan, are considered risky; some are considered less risky, as in the case of a mortgage; and others, such as government bonds and cash, carry no risk. It is a very crude mechanism. There were no ratings and no attempt at differentiating between different types of business loans. The crudeness, however, was not the main problem of the system. As long as banks played by the rules, the system would deliver a reasonable degree of stability. If the ratio of capital to assets was 8 percent, a simple calculation shows that the gearing of the bank could not exceed 12 at any time. This is a relative conservative value. We should not forget that the Basle rules, too, were the response to a previous crisis. And however sharply we may criticize those rules, they were indeed drawn with the best of intentions, with the goal to provide more capital adequacy to the global system.

Basle

The Basle rules play a central role in the credit market crisis. As indicated earlier, the discussion that eventually led to the Basle I Accord in 1998 was triggered by the collapse of Herstatt Bank in 1974. The central banks and politicians of the G10 nations (Belgium, Canada, France, Germany, Italy, Japan, the Netherlands, Sweden, Great Britain, and the United States, with Switzerland) were concerned that the banks lacked sufficient equity capital, increasing the risk of insolvency. Under the Basle I Accord, banks are required to meet specific minimum capital requirements. Under the ground rules of Basle I, banks are required to hold

(Continued)

equity capital equal to at least 8 percent of their risk-weighted assets. The emphasis is on the term "risk-weighted." The original Basle Accord included a highly rigid framework to arrive at this risk-weighted figure: Business and consumer loans were weighted at 100 percent, regardless of the creditworthiness of the borrower. Mortgages were weighted at only 50 percent and loans to other banks at 20 percent, while loans to the government were not included in the calculation at all.

Under the Basle I rules, banks were forced to constantly maintain their equity ratio at a minimum of 8 percent, which in turn forced them to manage their volumes of risk-weighted assets. It was relatively unattractive for a bank to keep loans to corporate customers with high credit ratings on their books, because these loans were weighted at 100 percent when calculating the bank's risk-weighted assets. There are critics who claim that Basle I was the real cause of the credit market bubble, because Basle I encouraged procyclical behavior. In the good times, when the value of assets rose, banks could lend more. In the bad times, when asset values fell, banks had to contract their lending operations to maintain capital adequacy requirements.

The Basle Accord deals with one type of risk only: capital adequacy risk. Other risks were not included, such as market risk and credit default risk. The failure of Great Britain's Barings Bank, in the mid 1990s, shows that it is also important to consider operational risk. Nick Leeson, a securities trader, had incurred such substantial losses for the bank that within days Barings Bank ceased to exist as an independent institution. These shortcomings later gave rise to the Basle II Accord, which became binding for banks in Europe in 2008, and for the United States in 2010. Under Basle II, the rigid framework of risk-weights was removed and replaced with a ratings system. Here, with the help of rating agencies, banks are required to rate their credit customers. In other words, corporate credit is no longer just corporate credit. Instead, risk-weighting now depends on a concrete rating of risk. At the time of the Herstatt collapse, many bankers had an unshaken faith in the quality of ratings. This is no longer the case after the recent crisis. One of the consequences of Basle II is that banks significantly increased their willingness to accept risk. As a result, one of the features of this crisis is that banks underestimated risk systemically.

On the one hand, the revision of the Basle I Accord was commendable, because risk is no longer appraised mechanically, and because it may not encourage banks to behave quite as irrationally. At the same time, it is important to realize that any such rule creates an industry whose sole purpose is to circumvent this rule. In this case, the industry was the credit market.

The problem with the Basle rules was not their crudeness, but that banks could circumvent them. Worse still, it was perfectly legal to do so. It was even encouraged. Textbooks on banking and finance used the euphemism of regulatory relief. This was probably the biggest and costliest financial scam of the twentieth century, and everybody was playing it.

The trick is off-balance sheet finance. Under accounting rules, a company or bank needs to consolidate everything it owns in its balance sheet. But this does not apply to companies in which the bank's own shareholding is less than a certain percentage rate, often 50 percent. The precise rules may vary from one jurisdiction to another, but all countries allowed banks to push assets off its balance sheet, and park them in a subsidiary, or, as occurred in this crisis, to shift those assets to the bank's parent group, which was not subject to the Basle rules. Remember, the Basle capital adequacy rules only applied to ordinary commercial banks, or to the banking units of conglomerates, but not to the conglomerates themselves. The rules did not apply to investment banks, or hedge funds, or other investment companies. Hedge funds were often geared 50 to 100 times, while the maximum possible gearing for a bank, under the Basle rules, was 12—or more realistically ten, since the banks needed some headroom. So the banks would, for example, create special purpose vehicles (SPVs), in which they would own a stake, but a stake below the ceiling, which would require the bank to consolidate the SPV into its accounts. The bank would then sell the assets, for example a pool of mortgages, to the SPV, in return for cash. How would the SPV obtain the cash? It would transform the mortgages into mortgage-backed securities (MBSs)—a process also known as securitization. We explain later how securitization works in all its gory detail. The mortgage-backed securities would be sold to investors. During the bubble, these securities were very popular among some investors, since they carried a higher interest rate than government bonds. And since investors mistakenly thought that real estate prices would go up forever, they did not see the risk that borrowers would ever default on their mortgages. The actual return on these securities depended crucially on whether borrowers would be able to service their loans. So these securities would be next to worthless once borrowers defaulted *en masse*.

When the bank sold a pool of mortgages to a special purpose vehicle, it would get either cash, or government bonds in return. From the point of view of the bank's balance sheet, there would have been a swap of a risky asset—the mortgage—for a nonrisky asset—the cash. The capital-to-asset ratio would thus be improved.

How to Circumvent the Basle Rules

Following is a simple example of how a bank could avoid the restrictions of the Basle rules. In this case, the ratio of capital to assets is 10 percent (capital divided by total risk-weighted assets)—comfortably above the Basle minimum of 8 percent.

Assets	$ (in millions)	Liabilities	$ (in millions)
Mortgage loans	100	Checking accounts	90
Total risk-weighted assets	100	Capital	10
Total Assets	**100**	**Total Liabilities**	**100**

Let us say the bank sells $20 million worth of mortgages to a special purpose vehicle in return for cash. This is what would happen:

(Continued)

25

Assets	$ (in millions)	Liabilities	$ (in millions)
Mortgage loans	80	Checking accounts	90
Cash	20	Capital	10
Total risk-weighted assets	80		
Total Assets	**100**	**Total Liabilities**	**100**

What happens to the Basle ratio? It has now gone up from 10 percent to 12.5 percent (capital divided by total risk-weighted assets). This means the bank now has more leeway to go out and sell some more mortgages. When it sells the next $20 million worth of mortgages, it passes this on to the same special purpose vehicle, or some other SPV. In other words, the bank has found a foolproof and totally legal way to circumvent the Basle rules. This is what is known as regulatory relief. You could also call it legal cheating.

For the banks, this game offered completely new opportunities. Whereas previously, the business of banks consisted of taking deposits while paying interest on those deposits, and lending money at a slightly higher interest rate, the possibility to offload assets to a special purpose vehicle presented banks with a whole new business model. It was called "originate and distribute," and it meant that the bank would turn itself into a marketing company. It would originate mortgages, which meant it would lend money, and then immediately repackage these mortgages and sell them to some off-balance sheet vehicle. In doing so, the bank would at all times comply with the Basle capital adequacy rules.

All this happened long before our recent crisis even started. The Basle I rules, which still applied during most of the crisis, were agreed in 1988. If it had not been for the rapid development of financial innovation and deregulation, Basle I might even have worked, or at least it might have worked for some time longer. Without the securitization boom, the whole idea of shoving assets into special purpose vehicles could not have worked. To gain a fuller understanding of the origins of our financial crisis, we therefore need to look back at the history of financial innovation and deregulation, since the late 1960s.

Deregulation

After the Great Depression, finance became regulated. Politicians and their economic advisors at the time wanted to make sure that this calamity could not happen again. And so they devised rules such as the Glass-Steagall Act in 1933 to separate commercial banking from investment banking, to ensure that deposit-taking banks would not play with the money on the stock market. The Glass-Steagall Act also gave rise to deposit insurance. A further financial innovation was the creation of Fannie Mae, to insure that banks would always be in a position to grant a mortgage even if the bank itself suffered difficulties.

But as John Kenneth Galbraith noted in his wonderful little book, *A Short History of Financial Euphoria*, the memory of a crash is short. Euphoria will eventually return. It always has in the past, and there is no reason to believe that it will be any different this time. The only remarkable aspect about the Great Depression is that it took a rather long time for markets to develop euphoria again. When Ronald Reagan became president of the United States in 1980, which almost coincided with the election of Margaret Thatcher as British prime minister, that post-Depression age of financial sobriety was ending. One of Mrs. Thatcher's first acts was the abolition of exchange controls. Her most important subsequent decision was the Big Bang deregulation of the city of London in 1986, which allowed big banks, both domestic and foreign, to buy up brokers, and jobbers—dealers who were registered with the London Stock Exchange—which gave rise to a number of very large investment banks. There was never a Glass-Steagall Act in Europe, and Big Bang removed many of the existing regulatory shackles, at least in London.

In the United States, one of the most significant acts of financial deregulation was the rollback of the Glass-Steagall Act in the 1980s and 1990s. The Glass-Steagall Act came into force in 1933, and it provided for a whole range of changes, among them the establishment of the Federal Deposit Insurance Corporation (FDIC) and the stipulation that bank holding companies must not own investment companies—the famous separation between commercial banks and investment banks. As memories of the Great Depression faded, elements of the Glass-Steagall Act were repealed bit by bit. The Depository

Institutions Deregulation and Monetary Control Act of 1980 repealed Glass-Steagall's Regulation Q, under which the Federal Reserve was able to regulate interest rates in savings accounts. The most important change came in 1999, when Senator Phil Gramm from Texas, and Congressmen Jim Leach from Iowa and Thomas J. Bliley, Jr. from Virginia, all Republicans, sponsored a bill, known as the Gramm, Leach, Bliley bill, or GLB, which repealed the separation of commercial and investment banks. The bill was signed into law by President Bill Clinton.

There was a big discussion about whether GLB directly contributed to the crisis. Former President Clinton himself believes that it did not, saying that without the bill, Bank of America could not have taken over Merrill Lynch in September 2008, during the same weekend when Lehman Brothers failed. Former Senator Gramm said Lehman Brothers failed because it was the least diversified bank, while JP Morgan Chase survived because of its diversification. Some economists, however, argue that GLB contributed directly to this crisis by creating moral hazard, and by providing financial institutions with excessive earnings.

To this author, it is somewhat implausible that GLB is a major cause of this crisis, though it probably contributed to the moral hazard on Wall Street, as have many other factors. If GLB is not a major cause, it would then be very difficult to pin our financial and economic crisis on deregulation, because this was the biggest act of deregulation there was. Another was the Commodity Futures Modernization Act, which was signed into law by President Clinton shortly before he left office. One of the purposes of this act was to deregulate some derivatives, such as single stock futures, and to provide a more open regulatory environment in general. But, again, it would be difficult to pin the crisis down to any single one of those acts.

Lax supervision is another matter. Failure by the Federal Reserve (the Fed) to supervise the subprime mortgage industry, or by the Securities and Exchange Commission (SEC) to crack down on alleged fraudsters such as Bernie Madoff almost certainly played a bigger role in this crisis than the few acts of deregulation. But deregulation and lax supervision are indirectly connected. The late 1990s and the beginning of the current decade were a period in which governments and regulatory agencies treated finance with kid gloves.

That was true even in continental Europe, where finance traditionally operated under much stricter rules. Governments lifted restrictions on entire market segments, such as the commercial paper market, which had been previously banned, or on the trade and selling of derivatives. Nobody wanted to lose business as a result of excessive regulation. Financial deregulation became a race at a global level. The United States and the United Kingdom were the front-runners in this race.

The New Millennium

Let's now fast-forward to the current millennium. In the 1970s and 1980s, the world created the Basle capital adequacy rules; financial innovation boomed; and everyone deregulated. China had long embarked on a growth model that would soon produce global imbalances, but not yet. That period experienced two large bubbles in the West, the pre-1987 bubble, the dot-com bubble in the 1990s, and various bubbles in Japan, East Asia, and Russia, which all burst with devastating effects. Japan suffered what observers would later call a "lost decade." Often they would say that something like this could never happen here.

Our new millennium started when Japan was on the verge of finally recovering from a lost decade. It started with a bubble, what else?

The predominant mood on the eve of the new millennium was that globalization and innovation would drive the world to new peaks. It was the age of unbridled optimism, in some ways reminiscent to the mood in Europe in the early part of the twentieth century, before World War I, which was also a period of calm before a very big storm. The first storm of the twenty-first century was the bursting of the dot-com bubble in 2000, and the recession of 2001, followed by the cataclysmic event of the terrorist attacks on New York and Washington, D.C., on September 11, 2001. It was a huge political shock that ultimately led to two Middle Eastern wars, but the much feared economic impact was relatively benign. On the contrary, the military and security spending produced a massive economic stimulus that helped the subsequent U.S. recovery.

The U.S. economy began to recover in 2002, but interest rates in the United States continued to fall as the recovery took hold. In 2003, the Fed cut the Fed Funds Target rate to 1 percent, a level at which it remained until 2004.

The period from 2002 to 2006 was one of extraordinary economic growth in the United States and in the world economies.

America benefited from what many observers believed to be a productivity revolution, caused by innovations in retailing, banking, and information technologies. Europe was lagging behind, but this was a decade of strong Asian, and particularly Chinese, economic growth. During this decade countries from central and eastern Europe joined the European Union (EU) and also benefited from very large capital inflows and economic growth. It is the golden age, as the president of Europe's central bank remarked. Ben Bernanke, who later became the chairman of the Fed, called it the age of moderation—by which he meant a moderation of prices—though in many other ways there was nothing moderate about it. It will probably be remembered as an age of immodesty, where bankers paid themselves excessive salaries and bonuses; an age in which asset prices went through the roof. In those few years, the world created another stock market bubble, a commodities bubble, an oil price bubble, a credit bubble, and a property bubble. The latter two were the instrumental drivers in our current crisis.

In Chapter 3 we will take a more detailed look at possible causes for this crisis. One of the immediate suspects, when the crisis broke out in 2007, was U.S. monetary policy during that time. (This author's view is that it was a contributor, but not a primary cause, but more on that in Chapter 3.) It is true, however, that in 2003 and 2004, American interest rates were below the rate of inflation. Under these conditions, economists say that the real interest rate is negative (more technically, one would arrive at this figure by subtracting expected inflation, not actual inflation, from the short-term interest rate). This means that money deposited into a bank savings account would actually lose value from one year to the next. Interest rates had fallen to such low levels, in both real and nominal terms, that it made more sense for any American to borrow than to save. In many ways, Americans reacted in a completely logical way to the incentives they had been given.

Why were interest rates so low at the time? The main reason was the fall in global inflation in general, and U.S. inflation in particular. The Federal Reserve feared in 2003 that the inflation rate may become actually too low, in fact so low that expectations of future inflation rates could become negative. In order to prevent deflation, the Fed cut the Fed Funds rate to a then historic low of 1 percent. This level was judged to be sufficiently low to insure that consumer price inflation would not turn into deflation.

Most consumer price indexes, including those used by the Federal Reserve, do not explicitly contain a measure of housing costs. In other words, the steep increase in house prices was not included in the calculation. What is included in the U.S. consumer price index is an owner's equivalent rent, an attempt to take into account the fluctuation in house prices and mortgage finance costs. House prices went up, but mortgages became cheaper, so the owner's equivalent rent did not register a similarly extreme movement. Asset prices shot through the roof, but these prices were outside the Federal Reserve's scope, and central bankers on both sides of the Atlantic agreed that they should not target asset prices. The theory was that they should clean up *after* an asset price bubble burst, but not prick bubbles themselves for a number of reasons. The theory was tested sooner than they could wish for.

Alan Greenspan

Anyone seeking a scapegoat could start with the central banks. The most popular scapegoat among all central bankers is Alan Greenspan, the legendary chairman of the U.S. Federal Reserve. Until he resigned in 2006, Greenspan was celebrated as one of the greatest central bankers of all time. But only a short time later, his former fans pointed to him as being principally to blame for the current economic crisis.

Greenspan himself is among those who were looking for a convenient scapegoat. He blamed the rating agencies. There has been a lot of finger-pointing in all directions. But the question of how much personal blame Greenspan bears for the situation should be addressed somewhat more critically than has been the case until now.

The argument of Greenspan's critics is as follows: The attacks of September 11, 2001 prompted an overreaction in both economic policy and the American political arena. Interest rates were lowered too far, to 1 percent, and were then allowed to remain at this level for too long. These extremely low interest rates caused the credit boom by making lucrative speculative activities like carry trade possible.

Critics were also outraged over what is known as the "Greenspan put." A put is an option used to hedge against the decline of a price or a market. The Greenspan put, therefore, provided speculators with the assurance that the U.S. Federal Reserve, in the event of a crisis, would help out investors by lowering interest rates. This supposed hedge led to an extremely high willingness to assume risk, which was ultimately responsible for the credit bubble.

The counterargument is that the Fed merely reacted to an extreme economic slowdown and the potential risks of deflation in 2002. Other central banks, say the proponents of this argument, would not have reacted differently.

But it is not entirely clear whether the blame should be assigned to Greenspan himself or to a larger group of economists who produced consensus in the United States. Nevertheless, the lax monetary policy of the Federal Reserve over extended periods of time did at least deeply influence the markets, creating a risk-friendly environment that lined the bubble.

The positions on this subject also vary widely in the academic arena. For instance, Irish economist Alan Ahearne wrote that the blame for the mortgage crisis does not lie with the Federal Reserve, but with lenders, borrowers, rating agencies, investment banks, and investors, because they all made money on the crisis, at least periodically. Others insist that there are deep causes for a market bubble, and that most of them can be found in economic policy. Of course, players and profiteers exist in every bubble, but the players themselves are rarely the cause. We should leave Greenspan alone, but it is legitimate to speculate on the extent to which monetary policy caused this bubble. It is also legitimate to ask the question of whether the monetary policy should focus narrowly on price stability or should price stability be defined in a broader sense. Direct inflation control, that is, the attempt to stabilize a given inflation index at a specific level or within a certain range, has prevailed internationally. The central banks have been very successful with this policy. But inflation rates were held down largely by cheap imports from Asia, and while the low interest rates did not cause inflation, they might have caused an asset price bubble, especially in real estate and stocks. The money supply also grew strongly during this period, and some skeptical central bankers and economists believed that the increased money supply, instead of affecting inflation, drove up the prices of assets. These prices are not included in the Consumer Price Index (CPI), which brings us to a reasonable question: Do the central banks focus on a price index that is too narrowly defined? Shouldn't they adopt a somewhat broader definition of price stability instead?

This debate is closely related to another controversy, which seemed to be have been settled by the 1990s, namely the question of whether central banks ought to control the money supply instead of inflation. This was the earlier argument of the monetarists, who postulated that there is a causal and calculable relationship between the growth of the money supply and inflation. But by the 1990s, this relationship between the money supply and inflation had fallen apart in almost every country, so that more and more central banks turned to direct inflation targeting.

The debate between monetarists and Keynesians, which had raged for several decades, seemed to have been resolved in the 1990s. It was clear that the monetarists had lost. It was only in Germany that the central bank, the Deutsche Bundesbank, was still pursuing a monetary policy based on control of the money supply, albeit with its credibility in decline. Even Milton Friedman, the godfather of monetarism, once admitted, in a moment of weakness, that the money supply is no longer an effective instrument of control. (However, he did change his mind again, shortly before his death in 2006.) The credit crisis gave new impetus to those who attached an important role to the money supply. Even if there is no direct relationship between the money supply and published inflation statistics, the rapid increase in the money supply, combined with an equally rapid increase in loans, clearly led to dramatic price increases in real estate and on the stock markets.

It is possible, then, that cheap imports from Asia motivated us to run too lax monetary policies for too long. And this overly loose monetary policy led, in succession, to a real estate boom, a stock market boom, and a credit market boom.

The global dynamics of inflation changed in 2007. Driven by rapidly rising prices for oil, commodities, and food—stemming in part from strong demand in emerging markets—the age of low inflation rates came to an end. It is perhaps no coincidence that several bubbles popped at the same time just as central banks worldwide began to raise their interest rates once again. Thus, the role of central banks in this crisis is indeed a legitimate subject.

The Property Bubble

The year when interest rates fell to zero, 2003, was the year when the rise in asset prices started to turn into a bubble, or rather multiple bubbles. The two most important took place in the markets for property and credit, both deeply interconnected. Let us first take a look at the U.S. property market.

The Case-Shiller Index for American home prices registered a 170 percent increase in real estate prices for the city of Los Angeles between 2000 and 2006. In other words, a property purchased in 2000 for $100,000 was worth $270,000 in 2006. Growth rates in other major cities for the same period were 120 percent for New York, 140 percent for Washington, D.C., and 180 percent for Miami. This means that home prices in Miami almost tripled within six years. Some European countries also experienced similar increases in real estate values, including the United Kingdom and Spain.

The real estate bubble went hand-in-hand with a mortgage bubble. Increasingly bizarre mortgages came to the market, such as teaser mortgages with initial rates that were below market rates, which, of course, would have to be paid for later on with above-average rates, or mortgages for amounts greater than the value of the underlying real estate. The subprime mortgage was one of the strangest creatures ever invented. It should have raised red flags, but this was not a time when people cared about red flags, least of all bankers.

Everyone knows by now what a subprime mortgage is. Some people still refer to our crisis as a subprime crisis, but this was always a misnomer of what became a much more serious financial and economic crisis. A subprime mortgage allowed poorer households to benefit from the fast increase in property values. In turn, the mortgage rates on those were much higher, to take into account the increased default risk. But subprime sellers calculated, mistakenly, that a default would not have dramatic consequences, since the property value would keep on rising. The bank would foreclose, and make a profit in the subsequent sale auction. If you believed that property prices would go on rising forever, a lot of those strange financial concoctions actually made sense. It was all premised on the belief of permanent price increases. Economic history tells us that this cannot be. We have been there before, time and again. We can state categorically, that in a mature economy like the United States, there is never, ever a good reason for nationwide house prices to rise much beyond the rate of inflation. If they do, it is always a bubble, and never anything else.

The euphoria in real estate markets became so extreme that banks or special brokers often approved mortgage loans blindly without the applicant ever having to submit so much as a single document. Even after the bubble had burst, mortgage brokers were still running radio and television ads touting mortgages that could be approved within an hour, with no scrutiny at all, and made available within a week. This would change considerably during the course of 2008. But before then, a prospective borrower could simply stroll into a bank or a mortgage broker's office, fill out a form and be approved on the spot for a loan of half a million dollars—for a mortgage that, in many cases, would never be repaid. Some cynical economists referred to the loans as "NINJA—'No income, no job, no assets'—loans." Many of those loans were marketed specifically to the lower income population and ethnic minorities.

At first, the subprime scam seemed to work okay. The default rate remained within reason. As long as the real estate market boomed, this pyramid scheme would continue to function. For this reason, the first act of our drama did not seem dramatic at all. Interest rates and inflation were at all-time lows, as was unemployment. Productivity growth was unusually high. It was indeed a period that could easily have been mistaken for a golden age by people who lived in it, and who benefited from it.

Thus, this first act of our crisis was still relatively pleasant, as in a Greek drama. The goose bumps come only in retrospect. It was an eerily good time for the world economy, and an even better time for the owners of real estate. We could borrow money at low interest rates and invest it in real estate and stocks. The rise in asset prices easily paid for the interest payments on loans. In other words, it seemed rational to borrow money and invest it in high-risk securities or real estate. In the short run, you would make a profit, for as long as asset prices went up. Finance became a seemingly self-sustaining activity. You could get rich by borrowing, and put the money into all kinds of risky assets, whether it was a house, a stock, a commodity, or an emerging market fund. The riskier, the better.

In a typical real estate bubble, people overborrow, the assets decline in value, and the banks sit on collateral with falling value. The Japanese experience, as well as the United Kingdom's banking crisis in the 1970s taught us that a simple real estate bubble can cause serious problems for the economy and the banking system. But our current story would be very different.

In our case the crisis was amplified by the credit market, which acted like a giant global amplifier. Mortgages were repackaged into mortgage-backed securities, which in turn were repackaged into even more complicated products, which in turn were sold to investors and banks all over the world. It is through the credit market that a national U.S. real estate crisis became a global financial crisis. Japan's crisis remained a national crisis, and if it had not been for the credit market, the U.S. crisis may have been much more contained as well. Now the United States is not only bigger than Japan, but it plays a much more important role in the world economy, so an American crisis would always have affected the world economy. But it was through the credit market that this transmission effect became so toxic.

It is therefore important to study the credit markets in some greater detail.

One important function of finance is to provide liquidity, and the credit market certainly managed to do that for as long as the bubble lasted. Through the process of securitization, prospective house owners were no longer dependent on their local bank. By selling a mortgage, banks were always in a position to grant new mortgages for as long as there was demand in the capital market. And right up to 2007, that demand seemed insatiable.

But securitization is not really new. It has been around since the 1970s, and the market took off in the 1980s. So what is new?

The big financial innovation in the 1990s is a proliferation of products to manage risk, which became possible through further innovation in mathematical finance. A whole industry developed to produce ever more "exotic" financial instruments, including some that helped banks manage their risks, and calculate default probabilities. The latter was at the heart of many products that were created in the credit market. Using a modern analytical framework, it was possible—at least the users thought it was possible—to calculate default risks with some degree of precision. These mathematical innovations produced a whole new series of products, such as credit default swaps, collateralized debt obligations, and even more complicated products that contained elements of various other products.

As indicated at the beginning of the book, I would like to present the nuts and bolts of these markets, the details necessary to allow readers to gain a more precise understanding of what actually happened. This is not a textbook of modern finance. There are many textbooks around—many now hopelessly outdated—that read like the cheerleaders of a world long gone. Nevertheless, a rudimentary understanding of the main mechanisms of these products helps to cut through the "toxic asset" metaphor, and allow a deeper understanding of how this catastrophe could have happened.

But before we do so, we should step back for a moment to think about what exactly is a financial market. We have already mentioned that one of the advantages is for borrowers to become less reliant on the health of their local bank. The instruments give borrowers access to a much larger capital market. In other words, these instruments provide liquidity, where a banking system might not.

The American economist Stephen G. Cecchetti attributes three functions to the financial market: providing liquidity, pooling information, and sharing risk. My colleague Martin Wolf of the *Financial Times* defines a "financial market" as a network of intermediaries between economic agents across time and space. This is a very good, though loaded, definition that expresses a significant aspect of modern financial markets, namely that it is not optimal to invest when money suddenly becomes available, but when the situation is most favorable for investments—and all on a global level. Ideally, the financial market ensures that money flows to where it is needed.

The financial market makes activities possible that would normally never exist. For example, it is not optimal for young people to pay rent for years, while painstakingly saving up the money for a down payment on a piece of property. It is better for them to take out an adjustable mortgage at a young age that can be adjusted to suit their circumstances at any time. The same applies to young entrepreneurs who should ideally receive a loan or venture capital, irrespective of whether or not they have a rich uncle.

Most people are familiar with only a small fraction of the financial market, the banking system and the stock market. During the 1990s, some of the modern products in credit markets were developed, which began to mushroom in the first decade of the new millennium.

The instruments in this market are debt securities, like government bonds, but a lot more complicated. Warren Buffett, who many consider one of the greatest investors of all time, has compared some of these new instruments with weapons of mass destruction. He would personally not touch them. The comparison is certainly exaggerated, and yet it is not entirely far-fetched. The instruments are extremely complicated and their effects can be devastating, both for the affected investor and for the economy as a whole. The truly horrifying aspect of these instruments is that many professionals have been willing to invest heavily in them without fully understanding them. If the credit market collapses, it is not someone's grandmother who is bankrupt, but her bank and the bank's reinsurance company, and possibly also the government that has to bail out the insurance company. Let's begin our discussion at the beginning.

How Modern Finance Works

The economic functions of finance have not changed in modern times, but the instruments have. The business model of banks has changed out of recognition, and so has the finance industry itself. The main players in the world of modern finance were the global commercial banks, specialist investment banks, and hedge funds. This was no longer a world in which banks lent money against some collateral, but a world in which everything became more technical and more complicated. It was a world in which everybody seemed to grow richer—the homeowners were able to enjoy rising home values; the banks were able to lend more without taking on new risks, and investors were able to buy exposure to exactly the kind of risk they needed. And the global investment banks, the middlemen in this game, were able to make profits that were unheard of in the history of capitalism. In this important chapter, we take a closer look at how this scam worked, in some detail. We need to dig a bit deeper to understand how the biggest financial fraud in history succeeded.

The Swap

The two most fundamental concepts of modern finance are the swap and securitization. A swap is a transaction between two parties, who agree to swap cash flows at a given transaction price. The dictionary definition is of limited value for explaining how swaps actually work. In a foreign exchange swap, two parties might swap dollars for euros at a given exchange rate. Of course, one can acquire euros on foreign exchange markets, but a swap might be attractive because it brings together two parties with opposing conditions and needs. One party has euros and needs dollars, while the other party has dollars and needs euros. They might both get a better deal through a swap.

The biggest swap market is the interest rate swap market, in which one party, for example, has a variable loan but wants a fixed one, and the other party has a fixed loan and wants a variable one.

Why are interest rate swaps such a big market? The reason is that small companies, for example, only have access to loans with variable interest rates, while larger companies are in a position to secure attractive fixed-interest loans in the market. If the large company prefers a variable interest rate, a swap transaction provides it with an opportunity to obtain the swap under very good conditions. The loans of the large and small company, in our example, are "swapped" according to a specific formula, and everyone ends up with the loan they prefer. The small company obtains a fixed-interest loan that would not be available under normal circumstances. The large company obtains a variable–interest rate loan under more favorable terms than those normally available in the market.

That is the rudimentary basics of a swap. The following sidebar provides an example of a concrete interest rate swap. In our narrative, the interest rate swap market plays no prominent role. We are interested in swaps because one of the most toxic products in the financial market today is a swap—a credit default swap, or CDS.

The Interest Rate Swap

Let us assume that there are two companies, Big Company and Small Company, and let us make the following assumptions: Big Company needs money for an investment. The following financing options are available to Big Company: LIBOR plus 0.5 percent, or a fixed interest rate of 5 percent. (LIBOR stands for London Interbank Offered Rate. It is a variable money market rate.) Small Company faces a less attractive choice: LIBOR plus 3 percent, or a fixed interest rate of 10 percent.

In this example, each of the two companies picks the option that is more attractive from its standpoint. Big Company chooses the bond with a 5 percent fixed interest rate. Small Company chooses the variable interest rate loan from its bank, that is, LIBOR plus 3 percent.

But Big Company would rather have a variable interest rate, under more attractive terms, and Small Company would prefer a fixed interest rate, but not at 10 percent. To achieve this, the two companies agree to the following swap: Big Company pays LIBOR to Small Company and in return receives a fixed interest rate of 5.2 percent from Small Company. Small Company pays a fixed interest rate of 5.4 percent and receives LIBOR.

The payment flows are depicted in Figure 1.1, both before and after the swap.

Figure 1.1 Payment flows (a) without a swap and (b) with a swap

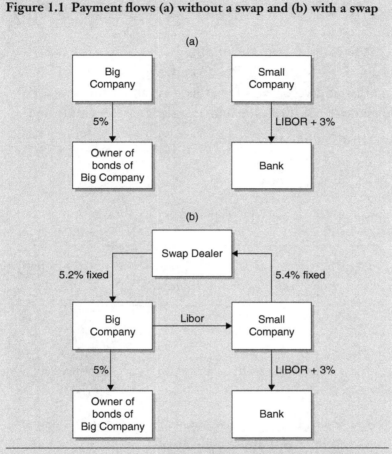

In this example, Big Company pays LIBOR, the variable market rate, to Small Company. Small Company, on the other hand, pays a fixed interest rate of 5.4 percent, of which Big Company receives 5.2 percent. The difference between these two fixed interest rates, in this case 0.2 percent, goes

(Continued)

to the swap dealer. In other words, the swap rate is 5.2 or 5.4 percent, depending on whether one is paying or receiving the fixed rate.

What is the bottom line for both companies after the swap? Let's start with Big Company: Big Company pays interest and receives interest as a result of the swap. Following are the interest payments made by Big Company:

Interest Payments:

For the bond, to the investors	5%
For the interest rate swap	LIBOR
Subtotal	5% + LIBOR
— interest revenues as a result of the swap	5.2%
Total	LIBOR − 0.2%

The following calculation applies to Small Company. Let's start with the interest payments:

Interest payments to the banks	LIBOR + 3%
Interest payments for the swap	5.4%
Subtotal	LIBOR + 8.4%
— Interest revenues as a result of the swap	LIBOR
Total	8.4%

As a result, Big Company pays LIBOR minus 0.2 percent instead of 5 percent fixed, while Small Company pays a fixed rate of 8.4 percent instead of LIBOR plus 3 percent.

Did both companies benefit? Yes and no. In both cases, the terms are more favorable than those that would have been available to the companies otherwise. As a reminder, in the market Big Company would have received LIBOR plus 0.5 percent, while Small Company would have received a loan at a fixed rate of 10 percent. Now Big Company is paying LIBOR minus 0.2 percent, while Small Company is receiving a fixed rate of 8.4 percent.

Of course, Big Company can still lose. If LIBOR rose above 5.2 percent, it would have been better for Big Company to have dispensed with the swap. Small Company would lose if LIBOR fell below 5.4 percent. Because one of these two conditions always applies, either Big Company or Small Company would lose relative to the terms chosen before the swap. In fact, both parties would lose if LIBOR fell exactly between 5.2 and 5.4 percent. The only party that always benefits, no matter what happens to LIBOR, is the swap dealer.

This simple example reveals the problematic nature of this instrument. Swap dealers, generally large investment banks, have a natural interest in *selling as many swaps as possible*. For the participating parties, a swap will only be worthwhile in retrospect under certain conditions. Of course, Small Company buys security as a result of the interest, because Small Company could face financial difficulties if the interest rate were to increase. This security may be more important to Small Company than the theoretical loss that would result if market interest rates were to fall significantly. Swaps are loaded financial instruments through which a great deal of money can be lost.

At the beginning of his book *Traders, Guns and Money*, author Satyajit Das cites a wonderful example of an Indonesian businessman who, on the advice of his bank, purchased

(*Continued*)

a dollar swap that he did not fully understand. He lost a great deal of money and sued the bank, and his suit was surprisingly successful. A favorable outcome for the investor is not always the case, however. Swaps are always complicated instruments, and investors should give careful thought to how a swap works under various scenarios involving different interest rates and exchange rates.

A simple interest rate swap is also known as a "vanilla swap." Bankers who coined this term may know a lot about financial instruments, but they know very little about vanilla, because otherwise they might have chosen a different name for something they consider simple or boring. But tempted as I surely am to discuss various varieties of the vanilla bean, I shall resist and remark that vanilla swaps are not the principle ingredient in our credit market binge. But they were the basic ingredient of another financial instrument, the credit default swap, which is altogether in a very different league.

Credit Default Swaps

When investor Warren Buffett called derivatives financial weapons of mass destruction, he was specifically referring to credit default swaps, or CDSs. The CDS provides investors with insurance against the default of a bond, which sounds innocuous enough at first. In some cases, the buyer of the CDS actually owns the bond, say a corporate bond, and wants some insurance. In other cases, the buyer does not own the bond, and uses the CDS for speculative purposes. If you buy fire insurance on your house, you would be expected to own the house. You could not buy fire insurance on your neighbor's house, and get paid when it burns down. In the CDS market, everything was possible.

In economic terms, the function of a CDS is that of an insurance policy. Legally speaking, however, CDSs are not insurance but traded financial instruments. As a result, CDSs, despite being insurance instruments, are not subject to insurance regulation. This, in turn, means that there is no regulation over whether those who guarantee the insurance are in fact in a position to pay it.

In our narrative so far, we have come across several types of risk: market risk, settlement risk (Herstatt), operational risk (Baring). The most important risk category here is counterparty risk. You are entitled to some money, such as payment on a CDS contract, but what if your counterparty cannot pay because it is insolvent? The author Nassim Taleb put this risk in very succinct terms in his article "Black Swan": "It is like buying insurance on the Titanic from someone on the Titanic."[1] In some cases, banks managed to sell insurance on themselves, which is an absurdity because the instant the insurance was triggered—the bank's bankruptcy—was also the same instance when the bank could *not* pay the insurance. The really interesting thing was not so much that someone would try to sell insurance on the Titanic, but that people actually bought it.

---

[1] Nassim Taleb, "Black Swan Investors Post Gains as Markets Take Dive," Bloomberg, Oct. 14, 2008, http://www.bloomberg.com/apps/news?pid=20601087&sid=aDVgqxiT9RSg&refer=home

The author Satyajit Das, whom we quoted earlier, wrote in his book that the insurance market is subject to the principle of *uberrime fides*, which in Latin means that both parties to an insurance transaction must treat each other with the greatest possible degree of openness and transparency. Under this principle, the policyholder must inform the insurance company of the actual risks, while the insurance company must specify exactly what is and what is not insured.

Countless lawyers have addressed the question of whether CDSs should formally be classified as insurance, but it has been decided that they should be treated as simple securities. Thus, a CDS, legally speaking, is merely an ordinary financial transaction. This explains why this market could become so large in the first place. Everyone was allowed to participate in what amounted to betting on insurance. Another Latin principle also applies to the market for CDSs: *caveat emptor*, or buyer beware.

From a purely technical standpoint, CDSs are swaps, in the sense that two payment flows are being exchanged. The individual insuring him- or herself against default pays an insurance premium once every quarter. The insurer pays a premium if an insured event occurs. Seen in this light, every insurance policy is essentially a swap. This is precisely one of the basic principles of modern finance. Through a combination of instruments you can replicate other instruments. Buying a CDS simulates insurance against default.

Let us assume that Investor A owns a bundle of GM bonds. Using a CDS, Investor A can insure against default by GM. To that end, the investor pays a quarterly premium to Investor B, who compensates Investor A if a credit event occurs.

How is a credit event defined?

There are several situations that trigger a credit event. Non-payment of a coupon is certainly a credit event, as is a corporate takeover or the nationalization of a company. The quarterly premium is calculated on the basis of a market price, which is expressed in basis points. GM CDSs, for example, might be priced at 500 basis points. This means that someone buying a GM CDS would be paying 5 percent (or 500 basis points) on $10 million worth of GM bonds. This would be $500,000 a year, or $125,000 each quarter. When we read that rates have gone up in the CDS market, this is a sign that the underlying bonds are now considered riskier than before. It has become more expensive to insure against default. The CDS market is therefore also a measure of risk aversion in the financial markets.

Who is the buyer in this market? Banks, of course, as well as hedge funds seeking to insure themselves against default risk of bonds they actually own. But as we were to learn later, many investors bought CDSs not to insure themselves, but to speculate. And who were the sellers? Among the largest were classic insurance companies like American International Group (AIG), which saw a seemly riskless opportunity to increase their profits. For as long as the property and credit bubbles continued, AIG and other CDS sellers did extraordinarily well, and it is no surprise that the CDS market itself became a bubble. It was an asymmetric game. During the good times, you rarely had to pay up, but you always received regular income flows. The more CDSs you created, the more money you would make in the short term, while postponing all possible problems to the future. However, that future is now.

In 2006, the British Bankers Association (BBA) conducted a survey about credit derivatives, which showed that the size of the global market had mushroomed from $5 trillion in 2004 to $26 trillion in 2006. These numbers alone point to the virtually unchecked growth in this market. Additional growth to a level of more than $30 trillion was forecast for 2007–2008. This is equal to $30,000 billion, or about 15 times Germany's gross domestic product (GDP). But even this forecast was too low. In 2008, the CDS market was worth $45 trillion, a number later corrected to $62 trillion. A year later, the market size was revalued at $30 trillion. This was probably the biggest financial balloon in history.

CDS indices are an important development that contributed to the explosive growth in this market. A CDS can be based on a single bond or an index of various bonds. In the latter case, the payment flows are clearly regulated. For instance, a CDS can be issued that offers insurance coverage for only the first three defaults in an index, while another CDS is issued to cover the fourth through the seventh default in the same index. In the accompanying sidebar, I describe how the prices of CDSs are presented and discuss the iTraxx Index, which is now Europe's most important CDS index.

Credit Default Swaps

The following formula is used to calculate the quarterly premium in a CDS contract:

Premium to be insured (usually $10 million) *multiplied by the swap rate* (in decimal notation).

Usually, a CDS contract relates to a bundle of bonds worth $10 million. CDSs are quoted in basis points (bp). A typical quotation for a CDS is 200bp, for example. This means that the annual premium is $10 million multiplied by 0.02, or $200,000. The quarterly payments are then equal to $50,000.

The CDS market began in the 1990s and literally exploded after 2004–2005, when CDS indices were first established. Like a stock index, a CDS index contains multiple entities. Let's discuss how a CDS index works.

There are several possibilities. In the case of a first-to-default swap, for example, the payment comes due when there is a default of a single entity in the index. Other possibilities include second-to-default swaps and subordinate basket default swaps. In the latter case, an upper limit is specified for each entity in the index, as well as an overall maximum limit.

Let us assume that the index consists of ten bonds. The contracting parties reach the following agreement: The maximum amount to be paid per bond in the index is $10 million, and the maximum total amount is $15 million. If the first bond defaults, causing a damage of $20 million, and the second bond defaults, causing a damage of $2 million, then a total $12 million will be payable under this contract—$10 million for the first bond and $2 million for the second.

The two best known CDS indices are the North American CDX index, and the European iTraxx index. When the media report on this market, they usually quote one of those indices. Following is an example of a market report dated September 4, 2007, in the very early days of the crisis, from the FT-Alphaville website, a financial industry weblog created by the *Financial Times*:

(*Continued*)

> *European credit derivatives markets weakened on Tuesday, with both the benchmark iTraxx Crossover index and the investment-grade iTraxx Europe index moving wider. By mid-morning, the Crossover index of 50 mostly high-yield corporate borrowers widened about 3bp to 331bp, while the Europe index added 1bp to 45bp.*

This report can be read as follows: First, two indices are cited. The first one is the iTraxx Crossover index, which consists of 50 European bonds that are rated as speculative by the rating agencies. The market report states that the iTraxx Crossover index has risen by three basis points, to 331. This means that the insurance premium against a default of bonds worth €10 million on the iTraxx index equals €331,000, compared with a previous premium of €328,000.

The iTraxx index, which relates to the bonds of companies with good credit ratings, closed one point higher on this day, at 45 basis points. The higher the quote, the higher the risk.

These basis points can also be interpreted as a risk premium. How much does it cost to obtain insurance against the default of U.S. Treasuries? A default event involving U.S. Treasuries is highly unlikely. U.S. Treasuries are considered to be the ultimate risk-free security. This means you would not pay a single cent to insure against default. Thus, when a CDS is quoted at 331bp, as the iTraxx was on September 4, 2007, it means that investors are prepared to pay a premium of 3.31 percent for the elevated risk. This does not sound like much and, in fact, it isn't. At the height of the credit boom, iTraxx premiums dropped to less than 150 basis points, which means that investors at the time were prepared to take considerable risks. This is evidenced by the comparison that, in March 2009, the iTraxx Crossover Index reached 1100pb—not too much tolerance for risk!

This leaves us with the question: Why do investors want to insure themselves against default, and why does anyone want to offer these insurance services? The reason for obtaining insurance has a lot to do with the fact that the modern financial markets actively manage risks—or mismanage risks, as it turned out. To this effect, banks use the knowledge of modern actuarial mathematics, which has developed sophisticated risk models that allow the illusion of precise risk management. One of the risk variables that is very popular among banks is called Value at Risk, or VaR, a concept from modern statistics that the financial market has adopted with enthusiasm. VaR reduces the broad spectrum of risks to which a bank is exposed to a single number. The fact that every bank actively managed its risks translated into a tremendous appetite for modern credit derivatives, including CDSs.

Some of the demand for these instruments does in fact stem from the need to hedge. In this regard, credit derivatives are similar to normal derivatives, like stock option certificates, which can be used to hedge against a decline in prices, for example.

As in the case of stock options, these instruments can also be misused. There is no regulation that limits purchases of CDS instruments only to owners of the underlying

(*Continued*)

bond. Many investors bought CDSs purely for speculative purposes—speculation on the default of some bonds or the rise in the probability of default. Remember, these were the days when people in the market said companies did not have the time to go bust. If you believed that, you would happily write CDS insurance. You collected a premium each quarter, for nothing in return, except a promise to pay up when the underlying bond defaulted. And since you believed this would never happen, writing CDS insurance was the closest you could get to legally printing money.

While an ordinary interest rate swap, for example, is, in cash flow terms, a zero-sum game, everyone seemed to be a winner in the CDS racket. The sellers of CDSs made risk-free gains. The buyers were able to take on risk insurance that was not available before.

A frequently asked question is: Why has this market only existed since the 1990s? Why did no one come up with the idea earlier of hedging bonds outside the official insurance market?

The answer lies in financial mathematics. In the past, it was not possible to determine a price for products such as CDSs and, as a result, they could not be traded. Similar reasoning applies to stock options. That market developed after mathematicians discovered how to compute stock options in the 1970s. CDSs were even more complicated than options, so that a new mathematical quantum leap was necessary.

The establishment of CDS indices was also tremendously important, because these indices allowed investors to hedge against an entire sector and not just against individual entities. For example, a bank issued a loan it had granted to a car maker, but it wished to hedge against a recession in the automobile sector. It purchased this protection by means of a CDS on an index.

Buying insurance seemed like a good idea. So why was this market so dangerous? It turned out that there were about ten insurance companies and banks that were the most active participants in this market. Among those ten were Lehman Brothers and AIG. If you bought a CDS from a defaulting bank, your risk insurance could be worthless. This is known as counterparty risk.

There are stories when banks sold default insurance against their own default—a logicial absurdity. Payment would be triggered by the event that the bank goes bust, and is no longer in a position to pay its bonds. But in that case, the bank surely would not pay its obligations of credit default swaps either. From the point of view of the sellers, this was probably the closest you could come to a risk-free transaction.

One of the reasons the Federal Reserve and the U.S. government rescued AIG in September 2008, was the important role the insurance company played in the CDS market. If AIG had been allowed to go bankrupt, many banks and investors would have suddenly discovered that their risk insurance was worthless. They would have had unhedged positions, which they would have needed to close immediately. It is not difficult to see how the default of one of those large counterparties could have triggered a systemic meltdown of the global financial market.

Apart from CDSs, the other three-letter acronym that played an important role in the economic crisis is that of the CDO, the collateralized debt obligation. The CDS is the explosive stuff. The CDOs are the toxic stuff. To understand CDOs, one needs to understand an important concept of modern finance: securitization.

Securitization

Back in the 1960s, the financial world was relatively simple. Exchange rates were fixed. Banks were banks, investment banks were investment banks, and the Glass-Steagall Act ensured that the two remained separate. There were no significant derivative markets at the time. It was not known how to price an option exactly, a problem that defied ordinary mathematics at the time. When banks made loans, they usually kept the loans in their own portfolio. An exception was mortgages, where the then federal government–owned Fannie Mae was able to buy up mortgages that met certain requirements. Fannie Mae was one of those many depression-era institutions, set up to ensure that market failure would not lead to a catastrophic negative spiral that would turn into an economic disaster. Toward the end of the 1960s, the period of old-fashioned banking ended. One of the major developments at the time was the privatization of Fannie Mae, and the securitization of mortgages. Securitization is a way to turn a pool of credits into bonds. The following sidebar discusses in more detail the concept of securitization.

What Is a Bond?

The most important basic financial instrument of all is the fixed-interest security, or bond. A typical bond is a security that pays a prearranged interest rate, or coupon, at regular intervals. At the end of the term, the investor is repaid the nominal value of the bond. Typical bonds are government bonds or bonds issued by large corporations.

Strictly speaking, a loan is not repaid but amortized. In other words, interest and a portion of the capital are repaid at regular intervals until the debt is extinguished. In the case of a bond, however, a strict distinction is drawn between the coupon and the capital value. This applies to what we would call a classic bond. Bonds can be structured in many ways. Another popular bond is the zero-coupon bond, which does not pay a coupon but offsets the lack of interest by repaying a larger amount at the end of the term. There are often tax reasons for such structures. Some countries tax income at a high rate but do not impose capital gains tax on certain privileged groups. A zero-coupon bond is structured to minimize the tax liability in such cases.

A bond, unlike a loan, can be traded on an exchange. What determines the price of a bond? One of several factors that determine the price of a bond is the market interest rate. Because the interest rate on the bond, or the coupon, is fixed, changes in market interest rates naturally affect the price. When market rates go up, the price of a bond falls,

(Continued)

because the bond is now relatively less attractive to what a buyer can obtain in the market, where interest rates are higher. To compensate for that effect, the price of the bond falls accordingly. For example, if the issue price of a bond is $100 and the market interest rate rises above the coupon rate, the price of the bond will fall below $100. This ensures that this bond remains attractive for new investors. In the case of fail-safe government bonds, the price of a bond can be calculated precisely using a simple formula. In order to apply this formula, one needs a few ingredients: term, coupon, purchase price, nominal price, and the market interest rate.

Because bonds are issued in the credit market by more or less creditworthy institutions, the creditworthiness of the issuer also plays a role. Government bonds are considered among the world's safest bonds, but that obviously depends on the government. U.S. Treasuries are considered probably the most risk-free security on the globe—though this might change as we move through this crisis. On the other hand, someone who has purchased a bond in the subprime mortgage market is exposed to extremely high default risk. As we saw in 2007, this is even true of subprime bonds with a triple-A (written "AAA") rating—that is, the best possible rating.

The valuation of risk is done by so-called rating agencies. The three best known of these agencies are Moody's, Standard & Poor's (S&P), and Fitch Ratings. The highest bond rating is Aaa at Moody's and AAA at Standard & Poor's. When it comes to moderate and lower ratings, there is more variety. For instance, a bond that does not meet its payment obligations is given a C rating by Moody's and a D rating by S&P and Fitch.

Rating agencies rate a bond by using mathematical models, market information, and experience. If a company's revenues are insufficient to repay a bond, the rating agency will lower the bond's rating accordingly. Government bond ratings are affected when countries are subject to political risks, such as the risk of a military coup or a revolution. For investors, ratings are a guideline, not a binding benchmark. Smart investors tend to form their own opinions, interpreting the rating as only one of many pieces of information.

Following is a very succinct description of the process that led to securitization. It is an extract from a handbook by the Comptroller of the Currency[2]:

> *Asset securitization began with the structured financing of mortgage pools in the 1970s. For decades before that, banks were essentially portfolio lenders; they held loans until they matured or were paid off. These loans were funded principally by deposits, and sometimes by debt, which was a direct obligation of the bank (rather than a claim on specific assets). But after World War II, depository institutions simply could not keep pace with the rising demand for housing credit. Banks, as well as other financial intermediaries sensing a market opportunity, sought ways of increasing the sources of mortgage*

---

[2] "Asset Securitization Comptroller's Handbook," Comptroller of the Currency Administrator of National Banks, 1997.

funding. To attract investors, investment bankers eventually developed an investment vehicle that isolated defined mortgage pools, segmented the credit risk, and structured the cash flows from the underlying loans. Although it took several years to develop efficient mortgage securitization structures, loan originators quickly realized the process was readily transferable to other types of loans as well.

Securitization is one of the most important innovations in modern finance. To understand the current bubble, one needs to understand securitization. Basically, securitization means assembling pools of loans to create bonds, which are then sold on the market. These bonds have different tranches with different risk. If you start from a pool of credit, of which you know that a certain percentage may default—but you don't know which exactly—you can structure a bond in such a way that one of the tranches is relatively risk-free while another tranche contains most of the risks.

The idea of securitization arose in the real estate industry, when Fannie Mae was privatized in the late 1960s. The purpose of Fannie Mae and Freddie Mac is to provide sufficient liquidity for mortgages, the purpose being to ensure that money is also available at times when the banking sector is not doing well. How do Fannie Mae and Freddie Mac achieve this? They buy up mortgages and issue so-called "mortgage-backed securities," or MBSs. Mortgage-backed securities are, as the name implies, securities that are secured, or backed, by mortgages.

Fannie Mae and Freddie Mac

Fannie Mae and Freddie Mac are very strange beasts. There is no international equivalent. Their origins, like those of so many modern institutions in the United States, lie in President Franklin D. Roosevelt's New Deal. In 1938, the Roosevelt administration created the so-called Federal National Mortgage Association, still a government institution at the time. The organization came to be known as Fannie Mae (based on the initials FNMA). Its purpose was to provide liquidity in the mortgage market. Fannie Mae was not a direct partner for those who wanted to obtain a home mortgage, but dealt with mortgage banks instead. It provided liquidity by buying home loans from mortgage banks, assuming the risk, and refinancing itself in the financial market. Using this system, the U.S. government indirectly supported the private real estate market for decades.

In 1968, Fannie Mae was privatized and transformed into a government-sponsored enterprise, that is, a privately held company with special government protection. Although Fannie Mae is private, it holds an implicit guarantee from the U.S. government, which allows it to obtain capital under the best possible terms. To guarantee competition, a competitor for Fannie Mae was created at the same time, the Federal Home Loan Mortgage Corporation, also known as Freddie Mac. In the industry, the two corporations are referred to simply by their folksy first names, Fannie and Freddie.

Nowadays, Fannie and Freddie still support the American mortgage market, in that they buy up mortgages subject to

(Continued)

certain criteria that are redefined every year, and convert them into securities, which are then traded in the financial market, the so-called mortgage-backed securities.

Before the current crisis, Fannie was the world's seventh-largest corporation. Fannie and Freddie were not responsible for the subprime mortgage crisis, but both lowered their standards considerably since the end of the 1990s, and took on ever more risk. When the crisis came, Fannie and Freddie were drowning in bad debt. By the summer of 2008, the two were effectively insolvent, and had to be rescued by the government. This financial crisis turned the clock full-circle. Fannie was back where it started in the 1930s.

Securitized mortgages are an important part of the credit market, but a lot more was being securitized in that market than just mortgages, such as car loans and credit card balances. The securities that stem from such loans are known by their somewhat more general name, the asset-backed security, or ABS.

This market was created in the 1970s, and it ballooned in the 1980s. It was suddenly possible to turn all kinds of loans into securities and provide liquidity for everything under the sun, not just mortgages and car loans, but also for leasing.

But there was another reason why this market expanded explosively in the 1990s and thereafter.

The reason is the original Basle Accord. You will recall that the Basle Accord required banks to hold equity capital equal to at least 8 percent of their risk-weighted assets. As a result, every bank in the world was given a credit limit based on its equity capital. But what happened when a bank hit this limit? Logically speaking, there were three possibilities. First, the bank was satisfied with its exposure, and left it at that. But a satisfied bank is a contradiction in terms. Second, the bank increased its capital, thereby creating additional latitude for new loans. Third, the bank sold existing loans. The third option became the rule.

The buyers of these loans are the Special Purpose Vehicles (SPVs) mentioned earlier. There is an alphabet soup of these SPVs. A particular type of SPV is called the Special Investment Vehicle, or SIV. In the following paragraph we discuss the generic SPV. An SPV is a company created specifically for the purpose of buying loans and then issuing bonds secured by these loans.

The SPV pays the bank an agreed sum for the loan. After that transaction the loan is no longer on the bank's balance sheet, and so the bank can issue new loans. The original loan is now held by the SPV, which, of course, is entitled to the regular repayments of the loans. The SPV has also assumed the risk from the bank. *The important thing is that the SPV does not appear on the bank's balance sheet.* An SPV is therefore a nonbank, but part of the shadow banking sector. An SPV performs the function of a bank, and yet it is not regulated as a bank.

This brings us to the next question: How does the SPV obtain the capital it needs for this transaction? It does so by issuing its own fixed-interest securities. The loans serve as collateral. The trick is that the SPV issues its securities in various risk classes, also known as tranches. The lowest level tranche, the one with the highest risk, is called equity. Equity is essentially a misnomer, because in this case it does not refer to stocks, but to bonds that are so risky that they share some of the characteristics of bonds. The mid-level tranche is called a mezzanine. A third, upper level, with the lowest level of risk, is called senior debt or tranche. When there is a default, the equity tranche is affected first, followed by the mezzanine tranche and, finally, by the senior tranche.

The opposite is the case with incoming payments. Whatever money flows into the loan pool, the senior tranche gets paid first, followed by the mezzanine tranche and, finally, the equity tranche. This is sometimes referred to as a waterfall, with the money being the water flowing downward from the upper-level tranches. The lower tranches receive all of the water that is not captured by the ones above.

What is the supposed attraction of this tranche system to investors? Unlike the loans themselves, the tranches are rated by the rating agencies. The rating agencies often rate the uppermost tranche as highly secure, because all of the risk is bundled in the lower tranches. The uppermost tranche is often rated AAA—the highest possible rating, which is normally reserved for the higher-quality government bonds. At the same time, yields for the highest-level tranches are higher than for government bonds. The equity tranche, on the other hand, carries significantly greater risk but has an extremely high return, which makes it particularly attractive for some speculators.

Figure 1.2 illustrates how a securitization structure works.

How does the rating process work? One of the surprising features of the system is that the SPV can essentially decide whether a tranche in an MBS will receive a rating of AAA or A. How can this be possible? One of the methods to create an AAA rating is over-collateralization. Remember, all these tranches are backed by a certain number of loans. To reduce the risk

Figure 1.2 Asset-backed security

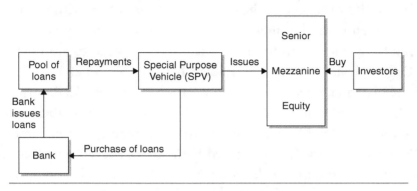

associated with a tranche, one could increase the number of loans—that is, offer more collateral than is strictly needed.

Securitization has proven to be an extremely important development in global financial markets. Before securitization, borrowers could only borrow if lenders existed. Markets are constantly drying up. Sometimes banks are more willing to lend money, while at other times they reduce their lending activity.

In other words, in a system that lacks securitization, a person who applies for a mortgage at the wrong time could find him- or herself out of luck. Securitization opened access to the capital market. This, in turn, meant that the entire liquidity of the global financial market was suddenly available. This, at least, was the theory. In our crisis, of course, the market for securitized products dried up, so that the global economy faced a massive liquidity squeeze. Some commentators have called for a return to simple, old-fashioned banking, but we should remember from the 1930s and earlier times, that simple banking was not exactly risk-free either.

The Economics of Securitization

It is useful to reflect on the economic aspects of securitization. A layman could be under the impression that money is simply being pushed from one corner of the market to another. Economically speaking, no value is being added here.

This, in fact, was also the view of John Kenneth Galbraith, who claimed that the financial market is wholly unsuitable for innovation. Paul Volcker, the former chairman of the Federal Reserve, essentially also agreed with that view. When asked what he considered to be the greatest innovation in modern finance in the last 30 years, he replied: the automatic teller machine, or ATM.

In the end, however, behind each transaction in the credit market, there is a loan, backed by some more or less secure asset. So is there also an economic justification for these instruments? Allow me to play devil's advocate. The proponents of the new world of asset-backed securities say that the modern credit market creates a more efficient allocation of credit than the classic bank market, where it was often the case that one needed money to borrow money. In particular, modern finance creates better access to venture capital for young companies. There is even a justification for the subprime mortgage market. Even though the number of defaults has risen, many subprime borrowers repay their mortgages. This means that this innovation in the financial markets made it possible in the first place for poorer people, or people with nonsteady incomes, to buy their own homes. In the old system, they would have had to rent forever.

In economic models, it is often naïvely assumed that everyone has access to capital. The reality, as we all know, is of course different. Thus, the economic role of the credit markets is to bring us closer to an ideal state in which anyone who needs credit can get credit—in other words, a state in which a truly liquid market for credit exists. Banks, on the other hand, create a lot of frictional energy in this system, in that they deny credit to a few good borrowers. Thus, the credit market performs the role of reducing this frictional energy.

Okay, it is not that easy for the author to say all this with a straight face. Let my devil's advocacy end right here. Whatever the purported benefits of securitization may have been, the damage caused by the excesses of the system vastly outweighed those benefits. Our crisis is to some extent a crisis of the world of securitized finance. So Galbraith was right. At the end of the day, we are talking about loans, nothing more and nothing less.

The Collateralized Debt Obligation

A collateralized debt obligation (CDO) is essentially a beefed-up mortgage-backed security (MBS). Remember, the assets of MBSs are mortgages, and the liabilities are the tranches. There is no reason why one should restrict the assets to mortgages only. You could, for example, use another MBS as your asset in a securitized structure. And you could put that new securitized structure in another securitized structure. This could go on indefinitely. In doing so, you could make the instruments ever more complicated. This is essentially what a CDO is about. Its collateral are not simple mortgages, but MBSs, or large corporate loans. Everything is bigger, and more complex. But the principle is no different from an MBS. The following sidebar provides a bit more detail.

A Short Primer on CDOs

Anyone who understands securitization in principle will have no trouble understanding the core instrument of modern credit markets. The "collateralized debt obligation" is nothing but a further development of securitization. Technical books often state that the CDO is a fundamentally different animal. This is not true. The principle is the same. An investment bank creates an SPV (special purpose vehicle), with the objective of converting a certain number of loans into securities. As with mortgage-backed securities (MBSs), the risk is divided into tranches, which are then rated by rating agencies and sold to investors.

How is this different from a standard securitized structure? The key difference is that a CDO does not purchase mortgages; it purchases the mortgage-backed securities themselves. Seen in a positive light, CDOs are nothing but a natural further development of MBSs.

CDOs are more flexible than MBSs. The types of CDOs vary widely. In the case of some CDOs, the goal is to actively manage the credit portfolio, just as managers of an investment fund try to optimize their investments. Other CDOs pursue very specific objectives. In some cases, banks are merely interested in removing loans from their balance sheets in order to satisfy the Basle capital regulations. As a rule, this type of CDO carries little risk.

This sidebar will not describe every ramification of the CDO market in detail here. Instead, the discussion will be limited to the CDO in its most basic form.

While mortgages serve as collateral for MBSs, CDOs are often one more step removed from the original borrower. There are CDOs that concentrate on certain security classes. Auto CDOs, for example, buy asset-backed securities that are backed by car loans. There are also CDOs that specialize in the bonds of major corporations. Most CDOs, however, specialize in mortgages.

Otherwise, CDOs work in much the same way as ABSs or MBSs. CDOs also issue tranches of securities with different risk profiles. As we saw in the last segment, the ratings are as good as the managers of CDOs deem them to be. In other words, a manager can apply the principle of over-collateralization to push a AAA rating. We already know that the loans serve as collateral for the issued securities. When over-collateralization is used, more loans are made available as collateral than necessary. The larger the number of loans that are identified as collateral, the higher the collateralization and rating. This means that it is quite possible to create a seemingly safe tranche from a group of risky loans, such as questionable American mortgage loans.

CDOs are not traded on exchanges, but directly by investors and sellers. In this market, a AA (read as double A) tranche, for example, might be offered at a yield of 8 percent. The risky junior tranche can even tempt investors with 20 percent returns. Depending on how high your appetite for risk is as an investor, and depending on whether you happen to have a need to shift your portfolio in one direction

(Continued)

or another, the market for CDOs always offers a product that satisfies the needs of an investor, based on its special risk structure and its returns. At least that was the case until the crisis erupted in August 2007. Many of these investors did not have to invest in the tedious stock markets, where most of them could rarely earn more than 10 percent. In the credit market, on the other hand, yields of 20 percent were commonly offered for risky securities.

Credit default swaps and CDOs were the drivers of the modern credit market. The coolest job in a bank was creating and selling those instruments. A considerably less cool job was that of a "quant," usually someone with a PhD in mathematics or physics, or later in financial engineering—people who work with a trader and actually construct the products, since it does involve a bit of sophisticated mathematics. The profits from this activity were mind-boggling, as were the annual bonus payments to bankers, especially to those engaged directly in the credit market.

Synthetic Collateralized Debt Obligations

An MBS is based on a pool of mortgages. A CDO is usually based on a pool of MBSs or major loans. The structure can be hyped up even further by replacing the loans with the CDSs discussed earlier. Another instrument used here is known as a credit linked note. It resembles a CDS, with the difference being that the seller contributes a portion of the insurance benefit from the start, which is then repaid at the end of the benefit under the applicable terms. With a synthetic CDO, the path from the borrower to the final investor becomes even longer and more complicated. The synthetic CDO is the riskiest and least transparent financial instrument in the credit market. If any instrument deserves to be called a weapon of mass destruction, this is it.

A brief note on the synthetic collateralized debt obligation: This instrument is very complicated. The synthetic CDO will not reappear in the subsequent narrative of this book. However, the following sidebar provides a taste of just how outlandish the structures in the credit market have become. In fact, one would be perfectly justified in asking: Who on earth came up with this?

The Technique of a Synthetic CDO

How does a synthetic collateralized debt obligation (CDO) work, and what is its purpose? A CDO can be used, for example, to pass on a pool of loans in return for cash. As we already know, banks do this sort of thing to obtain more leeway for their lending activities. Using a CDO, a bank can create this leeway without having to "sell" the loans. It can hold onto the loans by securing them with a CDS. As a result, the loans are no longer subject to the Basle rules.

This transaction differs from the previous transaction, in which the bank sold the loans directly to the CDO. This time, the bank buys itself coverage by means of a CDS. A synthetic CDO is established for this purpose. The bank buys the insurance coverage and the synthetic CDO sells it.

(Continued)

In other words, the bank pays an insurance premium to the CDO once every quarter.

Let us take a look at the world from the perspective of the synthetic CDO. It receives a premium once every quarter, for which it must provide a certain benefit in case of default. As with a normal CDO, these payments go to the investors. And like a normal CDO, a synthetic CDO also issues various tranches, that is, a senior, mezzanine, and junior tranche. But what secures these tranches? This is no longer entirely clear. The bank still holds the loans. The CDO has the credit risk. And the collateral consists in the contractual claim to payments from the bank.

The synthetic CDO does not buy loans, which raises the question: What happens to the money of the investors who buy the tranches? The money is invested in fail-safe government bonds, such as U.S. Treasury bills.

This is the basic structure of a synthetic CDO. In reality, however, all of this is far more complicated. In most cases, the structure includes the credit-linked notes mentioned above. As a rule, the entire credit risk is not spread across the CDO structure. Instead, part of the risk is processed between the bank and, for example, an insurance company in a separate swap known as a senior credit default swap. A super-senior tranche is created above the standard senior tranche. In addition, the banks often invest directly in the equity tranche.

There are countless variations of this structure. However, further details of the synthetic CDO will not be discussed here. Additional material on the subject can be found in the Appendix at the back of this book.

What good are these structures in the first place? After all, banks can also pass on their credit risk with an ordinary CDO. And corporate takeovers can also be financed with a standard CDO. The answer is that synthetic CDOs are an attempt to optimize the process even further, adding a significant amount of complexity, by offering the banks, that is, the customers, more attractive terms. The only problem is that synthetic CDOs are so complicated that it is no longer possible to properly calculate the risks involved. The real problem with complexity is not that we have to take the trouble to understand the products. Most banks understand all too well what it is they are investing in. The problem with complexity is that the risks can no longer be calculated.

There are other extreme variations of CDOs, such as CDOs of CDOs. These are CDOs that do not invest in loans, but rather tranches of other CDOs. They are also referred to as a CDO^2, or a "CDO squared." Not surprisingly, some brilliant mathematician eventually discovered the appeal of adding a third power, giving us the CDO^3. There is almost no economic justification for these products, except that they provide the investment banks that issue them with revenue in the form of high fees. In the case of a CDO^3, for example, the investment bank earns four commissions, one for each of the individual CDOs and one for the new, artificial structure. The gain, in the case of ABSs and CDOs, consists in the service agreement between the CDO and the investment bank. This is because the first loan payments go to the investment bank before being disbursed to the investors in the senior tranche—which explains why investment banks still did relatively well in the early part of the subprime crisis.

All it takes is an understanding of the principle of securitization to recognize most of the innovations in the financial markets. Everything else is derived from this principle. CDOs and CDSs, touted by many experts as the real innovations, are merely enhancements that do not necessarily denote progress.

As Alan Greenspan said in an interview with the *Financial Times*, not all financial innovations survive in the market. He predicted that CDOs would not be among the instruments that would stand a chance of surviving after this crisis, in contrast to CDSs, which serve the purpose of making risk more efficient. Greenspan's statement is controversial among experts. This author thinks he is right. There is a justification for a CDS market, albeit it for a CDS market with a different structure. The economic purpose of a CDO is much less clear. In any case, synthetic CDOs will almost surely not survive.

How the Speculation Worked

Armed with this knowledge of the modern financial instruments you are now in a position to consider an explanation as to how the speculation game during the bubble years actually worked. A critical player was the hedge fund. Hedge funds did not cause the crisis, just as no single player caused the crisis. But they were a great amplifier. Before we take a closer look at how investors used tranches of CDOs for speculation, we take a closer look at how hedge funds make money.

Hedge funds came up in the 1980s and mushroomed in the 1990s. They were often domiciled in some Caribbean island, which imposed no financial regulation at all. It was legal for those funds to be based offshore while being able to attract funds in the main financial centers where they also had large offices. One of the most famous funds was the Quantum Fund, run by the Hungarian-born financier George Soros, but over the years, this developed into a huge industry, with funds specializing in different types of activity.

The hedge funds were allowed to trade in derivatives, something that ordinary funds were not allowed to do. It was here, where financial deregulation and financial innovation came together.

Hedge funds are essentially normal investment funds, with the difference being that hedge funds make use of all kinds of modern financial instruments, whereas classic funds tend to buy or sell traditional securities. Because the former practice is not even permitted in many countries, most hedge funds are located in places with favorable regulatory environments. For this reason, many hedge funds are headquartered on tropical islands. The European hedge fund centers are London, Zurich, and Luxembourg, where regulation is relatively lax, at least compared with Germany.

In the 1980s, hedge funds primarily managed the assets of wealthy people, usually setting their minimum investment at $1 million. Not only have minimum investment requirements gone down since then, but classic funds, including pension funds, are also investing in hedge funds now, because many hedge funds yield higher returns.

How do hedge funds achieve higher returns? A well-known example is George Soros's Quantum Fund, which successfully betted against the British pound remaining in the European currency mechanism and earned $1 billion as a result. The trick consisted in short-selling the pound. A short sale is a sale of securities that the seller does not own, but which the seller must buy at a later date to legitimize the original sale. A short sale, in other words, involves speculating that the price of the security being sold will decline.

Short Sale

A short sale is selling something that you do not own. Imagine the following example. Let us assume that there is a rule on a stock exchange that requires all transactions to be settled within two weeks. This rule allows you to sell securities that you do not actually own, but selling them now, and purchasing them back later. Of course, short selling is only worthwhile to the seller if the price of the securities falls during this period. You incur a loss if the price rises.

A long sale refers to an ordinary purchase. You will encounter the terms "short" and "long" many times in this book. Short selling means that we are speculating that a price will decline, while long selling refers to speculating that a price will rise. Private investors are almost always long. Professionals are either long or short, depending on their assessment of the market. To apply the industry jargon to the Quantum Fund, Soros was "short English pounds." He was helped by the fact that there was a lower limit for the pound in the European currency mechanism. Soros executed short sales at this limit; that is, he sold pounds that he would have to buy back later. The central banks were initially responsive to his gamble and acted as final buyers. To execute his short sales, Soros first had to buy back the pounds, and he incurred relatively small losses as a result. But Soros had virtually unlimited credit lines. He continued to speculate until the central banks were no longer willing to back up the pound with support purchases. In the end, his bet paid off. The pound collapsed and Soros's short sale gamble succeeded.

Short sales played an important role during the course of the financial crisis. Bankers at Bear Stearns and Lehman Brothers, for example, assumed that the price of their stock dropped so precipitously because they were exposed to an attack of short sellers. They were the victims of something called a naked short sale, which means selling short without any collateral whatsoever. The short sellers were confident that they were making the right move. One of the first corrective steps regulatory agencies took in the crisis was to prohibit or restrict this form of short selling.

Short sales played an important role, especially for hedge funds. There are many possible hedge fund strategies. Soros was a so-called "macromanager," who speculated on the occurrence of certain economic events. However, this strategy tends to be the exception with hedge funds. The most popular structure is known as a long-short strategy. Someone pursuing this strategy would, for example, buy a company's stock (in which case, they are "long in stocks") and short sell bonds (making them "short in bonds"). In other words, this imaginary investor is selling corporate bonds that it will later have to buy back, in the hope that their price will fall.

The basic idea behind long-short strategies is that one is buying a security with higher returns and short selling another security with lower returns, and pocketing the difference. Such long-short strategies are not risk-free.

It is important to note that the long-short strategy is a standard strategy for hedge funds. Hedge fund managers are not particularly good at picking out the best values from the Dow Jones Index. This is the territory of private investors, although they are not particularly good at it either.

Another specialty of hedge funds is called the carry trade (which literally means that money is "carried" from one place to another). An investor borrows cheap yen, exchanges them into euros or dollars, invests the money at a higher day rate and, the next morning, exchanges it for yen once again, thereby earning a profit. Long-short strategies also play a central role in speculation in the credit markets. Long-short strategies can be used very effectively with the modern securitized debt instruments that later turned toxic. These instruments consisted of various tranches. And it was possible to be long in one tranche, and short in another.

Hedge funds achieve high returns in good times, but they can also suffer extremely high losses. The collapse of a large hedge fund can cause problems for other financial institutions. In 1998, Long-Term Capital Management (LTCM), the world's largest hedge fund at the time, backed the wrong horse by investing in Russian bonds, only to be faced with the Russian government suddenly declaring a moratorium on interest rates. LTCM used state-of-the-art mathematical methods and had two Nobel laureates, Robert Merton and Myron Scholes, on its board of directors.

In the good years, LTCM achieved returns of more than 30 percent. When LTCM got into trouble, it triggered such a panic on Wall Street that the New York branch of the Federal Reserve had to intervene to prevent the failure of LTCM from turning into a banking crisis. A number of banks, including Bear Stearns, had lent large amounts of money to LTCM.

Hedge funds, as investors, also play a central role in the current credit bubble. They were among the principal buyers of the highly profitable and highly risky CDO tranches. In other words, they are the customers. Hedge funds must achieve annual returns of at least 20 percent, because most investors do not invest directly in hedge funds, but in so-called "funds-of-funds," hedge funds that invest in hedge funds. The purpose of this strategy is to achieve a broader distribution of risk. But after the fees for the hedge fund managers and the funds-of-funds managers are deducted, the remaining return is only about 10 percent—the minimum acceptable amount. And this only works if all hedge funds in a funds-of-funds portfolio earned at least 20 percent.

Achieving a 20 percent return is not easy in a modern financial market. This is almost impossible in the stock market, and even more so in the bond market, where returns for ten-year U.S. Treasury bills are typically less than 5 percent. Of course, an important question arises at this point: Even if long-short strategies are lucrative, how is it that they can be used to make so much money?

The answer is leverage. If all hedge funds were long in equity tranches and short in mezzanine tranches, the price difference would eventually shrink.

As long as the price difference does not fall below a certain minimum, however, it is possible to secure a large profit by using the leverage effect of loans. Hedge funds do not just invest their investors' money. Instead, they secure loans for several times the amount of their investors' assets and then invest the entire sum. LTCM, for example, had a leverage factor of 30, meaning that it could invest $30 billion based on $1 billion in equity. Most hedge funds have a leverage factor of about five, but there are significant variations. Investors receive the profits from the total investment, minus interest. As long as the interest is lower than the return, leverage works. Otherwise, leverage kills.

What Exactly Is Leverage?

Many laymen are surprised to hear that bigger profits can be made with borrowed money than with one's own money. A simple example helps demonstrate how this is possible.

Let us assume that you buy a house for €1 million, in cash. After 15 years, the house is worth €1.8 million. The appreciation is 80 percent.

Now imagine you had financed the house with a mortgage. Let us make the simplified, albeit unrealistic assumption that the mortgage interest is zero. Let us also assume that 80 percent of the value of the house is financed with the mortgage, so that you pay only 20 percent up front. In this example, you would contribute €200,000 in equity, while the borrowed capital—the mortgage—would amount to €800,000. After 15 years, the value of the house has increased to €1.8 million. The appreciation is 800 percent. How high is the appreciation if 100 percent of the price of the house is financed with a mortgage? Because we would be dividing by zero, the product is infinite. You have turned a profit without any initial investment. However, such tricks are the exception in a market-based system. They can work, but only in real estate, where even ordinary citizens can obtain large loans, even without significant collateral, because the property itself serves as collateral.

But the principle is the same. The higher the share of borrowed capital, the higher the leverage.

But the game only works under one condition. The interest on your loan must be less than the appreciation of your investment, calculated over the same period, of course. In other words, if you take out a mortgage for 100 percent of the value of the real estate, and if the real estate market suddenly collapses, your leverage starts working in the opposite direction. This is precisely what happened after the collapse of the credit market. As long as money market interest rates are lower than the percentage rise in the assets you are invested in, a respectable profit can be made.

This is also the principle behind the carry trade. A carry trade between yen and euros, which takes advantage of the interest rate spreads between the two currencies, carries the risk of a sudden rise in the value of the yen, because the original loan must be repaid in yen. In other words, if the yen suddenly rises overnight, it is possible that the speculator, despite a positive interest rate spread, will no longer be able to pay back the yen debts.

(Continued)

> The business concept of the carry trade is precisely the same as the business concept of the private real estate speculation. As long as the speculators believe that they can achieve returns that exceed the interest they must pay, the concept works. The lower the interest rates, the larger the number of people who believe in the concept.

So how did the game work?

Based on what we have learned so far, we might expect hedge funds to simply stock up on highly profitable but highly risky purchases of securities in the equity tranche, in the hope that the borrowers will live up to their end of the deal and repay their loans. In other words, hedge funds would be long in the tranches of CDOs. This is not the case, at least not for most hedge funds. But it was the case for some of the banks that speculated in the mortgage markets last year. They were in fact long in some tranches that had been rated as safe. Pure long strategies, such as those pursued by inexperienced investors, in particular, are very risky, because the investor stands to lose a large share of his assets if the market crashes. The most risk-friendly investors did not work for the hedge funds but, to some extent, for the banks. For hedge funds, long strategies were too risky. They played a more cunning game.

Hedge funds gambled by employing the long-short strategies within a CDO. As we have discussed, there are three tranches in a simple CDO structure: equity, mezzanine, and senior. The game played by some of the hedge funds is called "long in equity, short in mezzanine."

This is very similar to long-short strategies in the stock and bond markets, in which an investor buys the highly profitable stocks of a company and short sells less profitable corporate bonds. In doing so, the investor is hedging against a shock. When a company encounters difficulties, both its stock and its bonds generally come under pressure. By pursuing a long-short strategy, the investor may lose money with the stocks, but will turn a profit with the bonds in the event of a crisis.

Hedge funds apply exactly the same principle in the credit markets, where they buy the highly profitable equity tranches and perform short sales in mezzanine tranches.

How can someone make money with this strategy? The answer lies in the idea that the valuation of individual tranches is correlated, so that, in this case, they move up or down together. This means that if one tranche is losing value, the other tranche will follow suit. The same applies to appreciation. If one tranche is doing well, so will the other tranche.

Thus, the lion's share of hedge funds bet on correlation. This is how the gamble works: If borrowers default on loans, the equity tranche bears the highest risk. This means that long-short investors will lose money first, because they are long in equity tranches. At the same time, they are also short in mezzanine tranches. Because they suspect that, in addition to the equity tranche, the mezzanine tranche will lose money, they offset their losses with short sales. In other words, they are hedging, or insuring themselves, against loss, which is fundamentally not a bad strategy. The investor ratchets up the return even further by using the leverage effect of loans. The strategy succeeds with surprising frequency. And when it does, hedge funds achieve their targeted 20 percent returns.

This strategy is based on the assumption that there is correlation between the tranches, that is, that the various tranches will always move in the same direction. This is a dangerous assumption, because it essentially contradicts the underlying concept of a CDO—namely that an undifferentiated mass of loans can be carefully divided up into securities with different risk profiles. In other words, it ought to be possible for one tranche to be doing well and another tranche to be doing poorly. If this is not the case, the entire setup no longer makes any sense.

It is perfectly reasonable to ask how such a strategy can work over time. Shouldn't we expect the returns on the various tranches to converge over time, especially if so many investors pursue this strategy?

In a normal market, such as a stock market, this would in fact be the case. But supply and demand conform to prices, and at some point the game would be exhausted. The reason this does not happen here has to do with the rating agencies and their models. The prices for tranches are determined by means of a mathematical model. They are called *mark-to-model* pricing. The model produces a theoretical price. As long as the banks are able to generate AAA tranches, a price difference between the individual tranches is guaranteed and, more importantly, fixed—until the rating agencies revise the ratings.

The rules of the market economy are essentially being completely ignored here. Prices in a market economy are determined by supply and demand, not by a price commissioner, a ministry of economics, or a mathematical model. If the latter were possible, the entire price-forming mechanism in a market economy would be deterministic. But this is not the case. Although an economic model can mirror an entire economy relatively well under certain circumstances, it cannot model each individual component. But this was precisely what was attempted in the credit market. In other words, we are look-ing at a planned economy of sorts, with the difference being that the planner was not a government but a computer.

As a result of central price formation, the price tensions between the individual tranches are maintained, regardless of whether demand is strong or weak. The game continues to go well until the rating agencies assign new ratings to the tranches. This was precisely what happened during the course of the mortgage crisis. The agencies began to downgrade their ratings for the upper tranches of subprime CDOs. When this hap-pened, the entire structure collapsed like a house of cards. The credit boom, in this form, would not have been possible with-out rating agencies. They are the ones that kept the prices of the upper, relatively safe tranches apart, even when the market, in a normal situation, would not have yielded such prices.

The long-short speculations in the credit markets worked well for a long time. As a result of the strong world economy, the number of corporate bankruptcies fell to a historic low in recent years. Loans became cheaper and cheaper. The credit spread—the difference between the interest for a specific bond and a "fail-safe" bond, such as a Treasury bill—reached historic lows. Some believed that innovation in the financial markets had eliminated all risk for all time.

This, of course, was an erroneous belief, but it does give a clear picture of what people were thinking at the time. The boom in the credit market led to small credit spreads, which in turn stoked up the credit market. Because of the rating agencies, the price range between the upper and lower tranches lasted longer than would have been the case in a normal market. In other words, what we had here was a form of perpetual motion that worked for a long time. But when it suddenly stopped working, it blew up in investors' faces.

This is also where we find the key differences between speculation in the credit markets and the stock market. One of the reasons lies in the market itself. Stocks, for example, can be bought or short-sold very efficiently. The institution of the stock exchange ensures that a market exists for stocks, one in which investors can trade at any time, regardless of whether or not buyers or sellers can be found.

This is not the case with CDOs, which are traded in an over-the-counter market. In other words, someone can only short sell in the mezzanine tranche if someone else can be found to buy mezzanine assets. (After all, the prices are not market prices, but "mark-to-model.") The individual markets, however, are often not liquid at all. Especially in times of panic, investors are often unable to execute their strategy. For long-short investors, this means that they are hit by the full force of losses in the equity tranche without being able to offset the loss with a supposed gain in the mezzanine tranche. In other words, the investors are not long-short, as they believe, but they are simply long-long. Precisely this scenario occurred in 2005, when the rating agencies downgraded the securities for the U.S. automakers.

Case Study: General Motors

It is worth studying an illustrative example of how long-short strategies can go seriously wrong—the case of major investor Kirk Kerkorian and General Motors. The long-short strategies of many investors were in fact successful for a long time.

However, cases of spectacularly erroneous speculation also existed. A prime example of how this sort of speculation could go wrong happened in the summer of 2005, when Kerkorian submitted an offer to buy close to 10 percent of the shares in General Motors. For many hedge funds, this offer represented a near catastrophe. It was a concrete example of the spectacular failure of a long-short strategy.

The major U.S. automobile manufacturers borrowed money through the capital market, that is, through corporate bonds. These bonds were then incorporated into collaterized debt obligations (CDOs), where they were arbitrarily tranched. As discussed in the previous section, the investors pursued the known long-short strategy in the automobile sector. The hedge funds were long in equity—that is, they bought the equity tranche—and short in the mezzanine tranche. In other words, it was a typical long-short bet within the credit market itself, straight out of the hedge fund textbook. Then two events happened almost at the same time that destroyed this bet.

On May 5, 2005, the Standard & Poor's rating agency downgraded Ford's debt by one level to BB+ and General Motors's debt by two levels to BB. The market's reaction was chaotic. The price of Ford and GM fixed-interest securities plummeted. The specific reasons for the downgrade are not of particular interest here, except to note that the rating agencies were suddenly less confident in the financial security of both companies.

Of course, this also made the CDO tranches less attractive. However, the hedge funds initially believed that they were hedged by their long-short strategy. After all, an event such as a downgrade is the reason a hedge fund would have taken this long-short bet in the first place. The hedge funds suffered losses in the equity tranche as a direct consequence of the downgrade by the rating agencies, but they hoped to be able to offset these losses by short selling in the mezzanine tranche. However, this didn't work, because the market in the mezzanine tranche was not as liquid as they hedge funds had expected. The prices in that tranche, after all, were *mark-to-model*, that is, determined by a mathematical model, and not *mark-to-market*, that is, market prices.

The hedge funds suddenly discovered that they were not hedged at all. To arrive at a functioning hedge after all, they sold normal shares short. In other words, they gambled on the expectation that stock prices would fall, which would have been expected after a downgrading of bond prices.

It was precisely at this point that Kerkorian showed up with his takeover bid. Although bond prices had fallen, stock prices suddenly went up because the market was betting on additional takeover bids. This was tantamount to a catastrophe for the hedge funds. After they had suffered painful losses in the CDO market, their next bet, this time in the stock market, was also unsuccessful.

In addition, the downgrading of the bonds, in combination with the Kerkorian bid, destroyed another popular bet. Prior to the downgrade, many funds were long in the bonds themselves (directly, not through the credit market!) and short in stocks. They reasoned that, in the event of a bankruptcy, they, as the holders of fixed-interest securities, would be entitled to a portion of the remaining assets, whereas the shares would be worthless. To inflate this supposed profit even further, many hedge funds did not buy the bonds directly, but rather sold hedges through credit default swaps (CDSs) on these bonds.

Following the downgrade, the price of this type of hedge rose, which signified a loss for the hedge funds. As in the first case, the hedge funds attempted to hedge by being short in the stocks. Kerkorian thwarted this strategy.

The lesson to be learned from this story is that there is no such thing as a perfect hedge. This doesn't mean that hedging is not advisable. In fact, the possibility of hedging greatly contributed to stabilizing the financial markets. But it is important, when calculating risk, to understand that no strategy comes with zero risk. Many investors in the American auto company CDOs truly believed that they were hedged. In reality, they were just as long as the naïve investors at some banks, who hoped to make a killing in the American mortgage market.

Warren Buffett once said that derivatives are like hell: easy to enter and almost impossible to exit. This is exactly how it was.

The Final Days of the Boom

The last full year of our combined housing and credit boom was 2006. That year, U.S. house prices stopped rising. Most participants in the markets had registered this event, but did not treat it seriously. It was thought of as a brief pause, nothing to worry about, and certainly nothing to impact the world of finance. The champagne kept flowing and the bonus payments for bankers would reach another record that year, as they would in every year.

At that time, there was little critical commentary. The newspapers showed no interest in the subject. Most financial journalists could not tell a CDS from a CDO. The media were mainly interested in the stock market, and the stock market performed well at the time. Stocks were where most financial journalism started and ended. At the time, only a few economists warned about the issue.

One was Raghuram G. Rajan,[3] a former chief economist of the International Monetary Fund (IMF). Speaking at the 2005 Jackson Hole conference, a prestigious annual conference organized by the Federal Reserve, he asked the question whether financial innovation had made the world riskier. He was laughed out of court by a number of economists present, including Larry Summers, a former Treasury Secretary in the Clinton administration and head of the National Economic Council under President Barack Obama. Summers called Rajan "largely misguided."

Perhaps the best-known oracle of the crisis was Nouriel Roubini, professor of economics at the Stern School of Business at New York University, who in 2006 began to warn that a crisis lay ahead.

Most economists, central bankers, and finance professionals looked the other way. And as for the general public, they had no idea that the credit market even existed. They certainly had no idea that it would soon blow up and so greatly affect their lives.

The first big shock waves arrived in late February 2007, by which time the subprime pyramid scheme no longer worked.

---

[3] http://blogs.wsj.com/economics/2008/08/23/a-proposal-for-the-banking-sectors-capital-woes/

The subprime game worked only for as long as house prices went up. It was through the appreciation of house prices, and the ability of the industry to turn that appreciation into ready cash that subprime borrowers were able to pay off their mortgages. In some cases, even that would not have been sufficient. Some of these mortgages were simply too crazy.

In February 2007, New Century, the second-largest subprime mortgage lender in the United States, suddenly reported substantial losses in the subprime business. Given the economics of subprime lending, the news should not have come as a surprise, but it startled the entire credit market. Interest margins began rising across the board, including those for CDOs that had nothing whatsoever to do with the real estate sector. The crisis briefly spread to the entire credit market. Borrowing became more expensive, and a sense of risk in the market returned, at least for a few weeks.

In late February 2007, the Shanghai Stock Exchange suddenly lost close to 10 percent of its value. The causes had nothing to do with the subprime debacle. Instead, it was a domestic Chinese matter. Shortly before the crash, the Chinese government had announced plans to limit speculation in stocks. The world markets used the panic in Shanghai as an excuse for a revaluation of global stocks. But it was a mini-crisis, and it ended within a few weeks.

Later, some observers would date the beginning of our crash to those events, rather than to the big freeze that would start a few months later. It was the beginning of the end, the first time the credit markets got a real scare. But this was nothing compared to what would happen a few months later.

First, the boom continued along merrily, and with it came increasingly more desperate attempts by market players to explain away the bubble with rational arguments.

Later in the spring, the bubble took on more ominous proportions, when a new form of credit became known to the public, a loan for companies with poor credit standing. As with subprime mortgages, the usual scrutiny was dispensed with for these loans. Normally, the maximum amount of a loan is closely related to the borrower's income. And a borrower is normally required to satisfy certain conditions before signing a loan application. Anyone who has ever applied for a mortgage knows that banks generally finance less than 100 percent of the value of the property in question, and that the monthly loan payment may not exceed a certain fraction of a borrower's net income. This is to ensure that the borrower does not become overextended.

But these precautions were dispensed with for this special type of loan. These loans were known as "cov-light," or "covenant light" loans, because they did not contain the usual protective covenants for the lender. In other words, cov-light describes a looser form of contractual agreement. Companies were now able to obtain syndicated loans for which they would normally not have qualified in usual times. In return, they paid interest rates that were somewhat higher than normal. But because it was such a booming market, these rates were in fact only slightly higher than market rates. From the standpoint of the investor, the return was relatively low in relation to the risk. However, investors, in their quest for slightly higher returns, cared very little about risk.

The controversy over these high-risk loans came to a head in May 2007, when Anthony Bolton, a well-known fund manager, publicly warned against these instruments. It is very rare to see such warnings coming directly from the industry, instead of from central bankers or journalists. Bolton's criticism was one of several warning signals issued at the time, signals that indicated that this was a market about to come apart at the seams.

At first, the markets also ignored this controversy. The credit spread, the difference in yield between loans and secure government bonds, was steadily shrinking. Investors at the time had completely ignored risk. A somewhat naïve fund manager once told the *Financial Times* that companies didn't have enough time to go bankrupt.

This would prove to be a colossal error of judgment. Almost the entire market succumbed to the illusion that there was plenty of liquidity available. But this is often an illusion. Suddenly something happens, and the liquidity vanishes into thin air. According to the old adage, you can always get a loan when you don't need it. It is the same story with liquidity. It is plentiful when it is not needed. For this reason, one should approach claims of abundant liquidity with caution.

Liquidity

Before the crisis broke out, we were constantly told that there was plenty of liquidity. Some claim that the reasons for the ample supply of liquidity was due to the low interest

(Continued)

rate policies of central banks, especially the Federal Reserve, from 2001 to 2003. Others say that the reasons lie in global imbalances. One explanation is monetary, while the other is based on the real economy.

We know liquidity when we see it. Defining it is far more difficult. Market players often learn the hard way that there is abundant liquidity in an upswing, and that it suddenly vanishes in a downturn—which is precisely what happened in this crisis. The reason for this is that deposited securities are worth less in a downturn, thereby reducing the credit supply.

Credit market expert Henry Maxey identifies three types of liquidity: cash, or liquid funds; credit granted on the basis of income expectations, such as consumer loans; and, finally, credit granted on the basis of collateral. Maxey also classifies the sources of liquidity, dividing them into liquidity generated by central banks, liquidity generated by the classic banking system, and finally, liquidity that originates in the nonbanking sector. The third source of liquidity plays an important role in the high levels of leverage for loans to hedge funds.

However, the types and sources of liquidity provide us with little information about the relationships among these groups. In other words, it can certainly be the case that liquidity at the end of the chain is a monetary phenomenon directly attributable to the central banks. Central banks provide banks with liquidity, which then inject liquidity into the economy through a series of direct and indirect channels. Where exactly the credit comes from, in the end, is ultimately irrelevant.

The causes of liquidity can also be global. Even when no blame can be assigned to domestic central banks, liquidity can arise when some countries, such as the OPEC nations or China, have large trade surpluses with the United States and channel the excess dollars through the global financial market. For this reason, a liquidity bubble is always ultimately an economic phenomenon.

These were the last few months before the crash. In June 2007, two hedge funds owned by the large U.S. investment bank Bear Stearns reported that they had run into serious financial difficulties as a result of the subprime mortgage crisis. At the time, it was believed that one of the funds was on the verge of collapse. The parent company later rescued the funds with billions in financial injections. By August 2007, the situation in the U.S. mortgage markets was becoming increasingly dicey.

After New Century, the second-largest U.S. mortgage lender, reported losses in February and filed for Chapter 11 bankruptcy in early April, the entire subprime industry suddenly began to falter. The decline in real estate prices accelerated in the second quarter of 2007, during which the Case-Shiller Home Price Index for the 20 largest U.S. cities fell 3.2 percent compared with the same period a year earlier.

Prices continued to slide in the third quarter. But there was considerable variability. In some regions, such as Chicago or the West Coast, losses were significantly higher. These numbers strike us today as comparatively mild, and they were. But it should remind us that it took as little as a 3 percent fall in house prices for the subprime mortgage industry to go belly-up.

These mortgages could not withstand a stagnation in the real estate market, let alone even the mildest of crashes. Subprime was the quintessential fair-weather construction.

In late 2006, many experts had predicted that the real estate market would soon recover. But in fact the opposite was the case. The price decline accelerated, and for borrowers in the subprime segment the implosion in the real estate market spelled financial ruin. Homeowners were suddenly confronted with a situation in which they could neither make their mortgage payments nor sell their houses, because the expected proceeds from a sale would have been lower than the principal on their mortgage.

The uncertainty continued in June and July of 2007. At that time there was a deep concern that a major hedge fund would go under, bringing down its own creditors in the process. A similar event happened in 1998, when Long-Term Capital Management, the world's largest hedge fund at the time, failed spectacularly after its heavily leveraged investment gambles went sour, triggering a financial crisis on Wall Street. In the weeks before the Big Bang, the hedge funds had attracted the attention of the entire world. But as it turned out, the market was waging yesterday's war, as it did so often. When disaster struck, it was clear that this was not merely a niche market we were talking about but rather a banking crisis first and foremost. It was not just another hedge fund crisis.

But at that time, it was not a crisis yet. It was like the calm before the storm.

The storm came in August.

CHAPTER 2

THE MELTDOWN

F inancial bubbles burst. They always do. When stock prices break through the roof, they come down eventually. The same goes with house prices. It is true that an individual stock, or an individual house, or even all houses in a particular city, might gain in value, and keep that value. But if you go beyond the level of a single company, a single house, or a single city, you are soon in a world in which nothing much happens on average, over time. What comes up, comes back down. That rule almost always holds—after you account for inflation. The fundamental law of house prices—known to almost no one during a boom, and almost everyone during the bust—is that house prices simply do not rise in real terms, even over long periods of time. Stock prices do go up, but no higher than a country's nominal growth of gross domestic product (GDP), which in industrial countries is usually no more than 6 percent per year. The infamous prediction of Dow 36,000 can only mean one of three things: a lot of inflation, another bubble, or an extremely long wait—a couple of generations.

While bubbles always burst, they do not always burst in the same way. Some bubbles start with a bang, and then the decline continues slowly and steadily. This is what happened in 1929. The famous Wall Street crash was only the beginning of the world's worst bear market in history, which lasted for another three years. The Japanese bubble did not end with a bang, but it gave way to a very long-term decline. The dot-com bubble at the beginning of our new millennium also burst in stages. The bubble that burst in 1987, by contrast, ended in a bang. After the bang, life quickly returned to normal.

Our credit bubble ended with a bang, but not the kind of bang that most people are familiar with. Nothing much happened in stock markets, in bond markets, or foreign exchange moneys. The bang occurred in a place that most people are unfamiliar with, the money market.

The Meltdown Begins

Nobody really remembers why it happened. There was no trigger that popped, no bank that reported difficulties on that day. It just happened. The bang was first heard in Europe in the early hours of Thursday, August 9, 2007, when America was still sleeping. Around noon, Central European Time, sellers suddenly went on strike in the European interbank markets, where banks supply each other with overnight credit without collateral. Because loans are extremely short-term, interest rates in the interbank market are relatively stable, generally hovering near the short-term interest rate of the central bank—the Fed Funds rate in the case of the United States.

On August 9, those money market interest rates suddenly jumped up. This is very unusual. In Europe, the central bank's official interest rate had been 4 percent at the time. It was 5.25 percent in the United States. But the European overnight money market rates suddenly jumped up to over 4.4 percent. It seemed that money was becoming scarce in the money market. Banks were suddenly no longer willing to lend money to each other. Ensuring stable conditions in the money markets is one of the tasks of a central bank, and so the European Central Bank intervened to a previously unheard-of extent, providing the market with liquidity worth €95 billion within a very short time. When Wall Street opened on August 9, the same happened there when the Federal Reserve, using two money market operations, pumped a total of $24 billion into the market. It was not a local crisis. The money markets had decoupled everywhere, and central banks everywhere were trying to inject liquidity into the system.

The following sidebar gives some technical details about banks and central banks, and how they provide liquidity in the money market and the economy.

Some Elementary Background on Central Banks

One of the main functions of a central bank is to provide banks with liquidity. Before central banks existed, there were privileged private banks that were entitled to disburse money, as well as clearinghouses maintained by the banks themselves that managed payment transactions between banks and served as lenders of last resort. Nowadays we have

(Continued)

national central banks, usually institutions that are independent of governments, which control the money supply. Their primary function is to guarantee the stability of money and the financial sector.

How does money get from the central bank to the commercial banks? In the United States, commercial banks maintain reserve accounts with the Federal Reserve (the Fed). How much depends on several factors, including the amount the banks have lent to customers. It is usually around 10 percent of the bank's demand accounts—the accounts that could be closed at any time. To manage their reserve accounts with the Fed, banks use the Fed Funds market overnight. If a bank has insufficient reserves, it can borrow from another bank at a privately agreed interest rate. The average of those rates is known as the Fed Funds rate. The Fed does not determine this rate directly, but indirectly through open market operations. The interest rate the Fed sets is called the Fed Funds Target rate. How does the Fed insure that the target rate becomes the actual rate? It does so by open market operations. This means the Fed buys or sells securities, mostly Treasury bonds, to and from the banks. In that process, the banks' reserves accounts with the Fed go up or down, and that directly influences the interest rate.

There have been occasions, such as in the fall of 2008, when the Fed allowed the Funds Market rate to deviate from its target rate. The actual funds rate fell to zero some time before the official target rate did.

In Europe, the system works a little differently. There, the European Central Bank (ECB) injects money into the markets using something called a securities repurchase agreement, or repo. Under these agreements, central banks lend money to individual banks for a period of two weeks, in return for securities, but only those that are accepted by the central bank. They include, for example, government bonds. In the end, the banks repay the loans and get the securities back—hence "repurchase agreement." This process takes place through a so-called "tender," or "auction," in which the central bank sets a minimum interest rate, or a fixed rate. This minimum or fixed rate is known as the repo rate. When we read in the newspapers that the Fed or the ECB have cut rates, it means that the Fed has lowered the Fed Fund Target rate, and the ECB has lowered its repo rate. They are not the same rates. But as long as money markets worked efficiently, there was never a reason for the general public, even for economists, to be particularly bothered about short-term interest rates. They were all essentially the same, and the central bank determined what it was. That was no longer the case after the crisis.

To obtain money from the central bank via repos, banks must provide the corresponding collateral. The central bank decides what kinds of securities are allowable, a decision that represents an important control instrument in times of crisis. When banks hold securities that they cannot sell in the market, a central bank's decision as to whether or not to accept these securities as collateral can be critical to the banks' ability to survive. This was a central issue in this credit crisis, when central banks began accepting collateral of a lower quality than was standard practice. They did not accept subprime mortgage securities, but there were lots of other securities that banks were able to offload in exchange for instant liquidity.

Central banks have used all avenues available to them to inject liquidity into the banking system. Most central banks have some form of emergency lending rate, at which banks can borrow overnight without collateral, but at a higher rate. In the United States, this rate is known as the discount rate. (This is another example where you should not apply common sense to financial terms. There is a technical reason for the use of the term "discount," but from the bank's point of view, the interest rate is not at a discount to the market, but at a premium.) Such emergency financing through a central bank is costly and often embarrassing for banks. Banks are loath to admit that they have borrowed money from a central bank outside the normal process, because such information is usually public. The U.S. economist Stephen Cecchetti, now the chief economist of the Bank of International Settlements, once compared this operation with borrowing money from one's parents, but in such a way that all your friends know that you have just borrowed money from your parents. In the case of the banks, however, this is not vanity—this is survival. Once other banks realize you are in trouble, they stop lending to you, and as a result, you are in even more trouble.

However, in normal times, the bulk of routine refinancing takes place in the interbank markets, not through the central bank. In the interbank market, banks lend each other money—without collateral. Interest rates in the interbank market are generally very close to the official central bank rates. But when a credit crunch occurs, these rates can rise more quickly, which is precisely what happened in August 2007, and continues to the present.

The relevant interest rate in the U.S. money market is the overnight LIBOR, which stands for London Interbank Offered Rate. Many loans with variable interest rates are based on the LIBOR, for example, the three-month LIBOR. A typical loan is sometimes calculated as LIBOR plus 200 basis points (where 100 basis points equal one percent). In the European market, the relevant rate is called EONIA, the European Overnight Interest Average.

During the crisis, the central banks intervened to provide the banks with sufficient liquidity, because the interbank market had collapsed. The interventions became increasingly significant, and yet the central banks failed to stabilize the money markets, irrespective of how much money they pumped into the system. The problem was that banks had lost confidence in the entire system. They knew their own positions, or thought they did, and they suspected other banks were in just the same trouble, or worse. So there was a lot of liquidity in the system as a whole, but banks hoarded the cash. They did not lend the surplus liquidity in the money market, nor did they lend to the usual customers—or at least not in the quantities they used to.

The central bank interventions, however, were successful in one important respect. There were no bank runs as there were during 1907 or 1929. There was one notable exception, which occurred in the United Kingdom. Northern Rock, a

(Continued)

mortgage bank, or "building society" as they call it there, was subject to a bank run in September 2007, when customers stood in line for hours to close their accounts. The bank was one of the most competitive institutions during the property bubble, offering mortgages at lower interest rates, in some cases up to 130 percent of the property's value. But Northern Rock was an exception, which was caused by particularly inept handling by the government, and by the lack of an effective deposit insurance scheme. In the United States, and in most other countries, deposit insurance has been in place, so that banks are much safer than they were in the past.

In fact, the central banks intervened not just that day, but day after day after day for several months. This first round of interventions failed to stabilize the money market. The interest rate spread increased permanently. Money market interest rates were just half a percentage point above base rates around the world. A worldwide liquidity problem had developed.

The ever optimistic Wall Street establishment had hoped that this horrific episode would pass quickly, but the situation only deteriorated further. The liquidity crisis in the interbank market spilled over into another segment of the money market, the market for commercial paper.

The Crisis Spreads to All Segments of the Money Market

Commercial paper is part of the money market. Large companies often use commercial paper to obtain short-term funds. Like the interbank market, this is a market with no collateral, similar to a bond market, except that the duration is much shorter. There was a special subsegment of this market, known as the asset-backed commercial paper market. This was a market in which players other than large companies could raise short-term funds by pledging collateral.

Earlier we discussed SPVs, or Special Purpose Vehicles. They are the sausage factories of the credit market. There are also Special Investment Vehicles (SIVs), or conduits. There are subtle, technical differences between these terms. And then there is the structure known as the SIV-light. Without getting into the technical details, SIV-lights are financed through asset-backed commercial paper (ABCP). And when this subsegment of the commercial paper market shut down, those companies were in trouble. Long-term financing was no longer functioning, because investors no longer wanted to buy the securities, and short-term financing also wasn't working, because the money market wouldn't accept these securities as sufficient collateral. This led to an acute financial crisis among some of these companies. They were stuck with securities that no one wanted, not even the ABCP market, where they could usually serve as collateral.

In other words, at this point the crisis had encompassed almost the entire money market. Even though the SPVs do not belong to the banks, the banks are still liable for their losses, because the SPVs were usually owned by the banks' holding companies. This led to the various mini-crises among the banks, first at Bear Stearns, then at various other banks around the world. Banks like Citibank, Bank of America, and Deutsche Bank, as well as some investment banks like Merrill Lynch, had suffered losses in the billions, which they began to write off in the third quarter. The CEOs of Merrill Lynch and Citibank were later forced to resign. The problem, throughout this entire period, was that hardly anyone knew where the bottom of the barrel was. New catastrophic reports were added to the mix every day.

What the investors did not take into account was the fact that they were investing in markets in which liquidity was not guaranteed. Of course, there was a lot of liquidity when times were good, but that changed very quickly when the banks discovered that there were no longer any buyers for these securities. The market would have been able to tolerate a short-term strike on the part of buyers, but the high level of default on American subprime mortgages meant that the value of the securities held by the banks had in fact declined. When the crisis erupted, many of these securities were practically worthless.

The Banks Were Hit First—Not the Hedge Funds

When the crisis erupted, the big fear was that the shadow banking system—the investment banks, the hedge funds, the SIVs—would all go belly-up bringing down the entire financial system. What people at the time did not realize was that the commercial banks themselves were in trouble. They were forced by their regulators to consolidate their SPVs and SIVs. In some cases, banks directly held those securities in long position. This is what was perhaps the most surprising aspect of the crisis. The hedge funds often got it wrong with long-short strategies, as we have just seen. But at least they were not long all tranches of credit. There were banks, in Europe in particular, and other investors, who simply bought the stuff. Australian investors, apparently, had a liking for mezzanine tranches. Now, some of the senior tranches turned out to be relatively safe, but the equity and mezzanine tranches were real junk. Of course, during the good times the interest on these tranches was handsome. But just buying the stuff without a hedge seemed irresponsible, even by the reckless standards of the time. And the most irresponsible participants in the financial system were not the hedge funds, but the banks.

Traditional funds are also involved in this business. According to the *Financial Times*, an internal survey conducted at Citibank revealed that the principal buyers of the equity tranche of collateralized debt obligations, or CDOs, were not hedge funds, as would have been expected, but classic mutual funds and even pension funds. In other words, those funds that were once risk-averse were suddenly willing to engage in highly risky gambles. This sort of thing is usually a sign of an impending crash (not unlike the observation made by Joseph Kennedy, President John F. Kennedy's father, who sold his shares ahead of the stock market crash in 1929 after getting stock tips from his shoeshine boys). During the bubble, classic funds were just as much of a gamble as some of the speculative funds, the only difference being that many fund managers did not understand the products and the risk as well as some hedge fund professionals.

Everyone Hates the Credit Rating Agencies

In August 2007, our Great Crisis began, and it was still there in September, when people registered with surprise that the situation had been allowed to persist for a whole month. Little idea did they have that this was just the beginning. By that time, however, the finger pointing had already begun, and it is no surprise that the rating agencies initially took most of the blame. In the causal chain of events, they were the closest culprits. For decades, the three well-known rating agencies, Moody's, Standard & Poor's, and Fitch Ratings, played the role of referees in the financial system, and during the bubble they became active players. Rating agencies issue ratings for bonds, including the tranches of CDOs and mortgage-backed securities, or MBSs. U.S. Treasuries enjoy the highest rating, AAA, or "triple A," which corresponds to a three-star Michelin rating. Triple A signifies that the risk of default is so low that it is in fact negligible. While this is indeed the case with U.S. Treasuries, it was, unfortunately, not true of all AAA-rated securities. As Lloyd Blankfein, the head of Goldman Sachs, once remarked, there are only a very small number of AAA-rated companies in the world, but some 60,000 bonds classified as AAA. Surely, this cannot be right.

Rating agencies are not nonprofit or government institutions, but companies that earn profits with the ratings. Of course, these companies are not open to bribery, though there have been some disturbing reports about irregularities. But the real problem was not any alleged wrongdoing, but the way the system worked in its normal, above-the-board legal way. The way the rating system operated, for example the practice of over-collateralization, raised considerable doubts.

Rating agencies base their ratings on models, market information, and experience. In the case of credit derivatives and CDOs, however, it is impossible to conclude, based on experience, when a specific borrower will go under. This leaves the agencies with nothing but mathematical models to work with. As a result, rating agencies issued AAA ratings for the senior tranches of risky CDOs on the strength of the mathematically calculated probability that this tranche constituted a risk. These models gave rise to the logic-defying of the credit market, that it was possible to create good securities from bad loans. As I will argue in the next chapter, this is partly attributable to the fact that the models are systemically wrong. Critics of the rating agencies argue that they caused this bubble with their high ratings. Without these ratings, the credit market racket could not have functioned.

A typical incident that occurred in 2007 sheds a lot of light on the behavior of the rating agencies. Moody's upgraded its ratings of the three major Icelandic banks to AAA with the argument that the Icelandic government would intervene if a banking crisis occurred. With hindsight we know what happened. The banks did indeed go bust, and Iceland did indeed bail them out, but in the process the country itself went *de facto* bankrupt. With such silly maneuvers, the rating agencies were at least partly responsible for placing themselves at the center of the criticism.

After the collapse of the credit markets in 2007, the blame game began. In the subprime market, even the prices of AAA-rated CDOs fell dramatically. The rating system was completely discredited, and the rating agencies were placed at the top of everyone's hit list.

The rating agencies have defended their role. They said their valuation standards are transparent and obvious to anyone. Nevertheless, the question arises as to whether a system that consists of the ratings and valuations of a small group of private companies is optimal. When the crisis began, efforts were underway, spearheaded in part by Germany in its role as holder of the rotating presidency of the G-7, the Group of Seven—United States, Germany, Japan, France, Great Britain, Italy, and Canada—to impose stricter regulations on the rating agencies. Others are proposing to take them out of the equation altogether, by persuading governments and central banks no longer to rely on ratings in any official capacity. We will discuss these proposals in the final chapter.

No matter how one feels about the subject of regulating the rating agencies, it would be wrong to hold them solely responsible for the credit market crisis, as Alan Greenspan did in September 2007, just as it is wrong to blame Alan Greenspan. The rating agencies were certainly among the players that raked in handsome profits as a result of the bubble. The ratings certainly played a role when it came to selling exceedingly complex products to exceedingly ignorant investors, who understood nothing about the product aside from the ratings. In this respect, the rating agencies are culpable. No matter what happens now, whether there is going to be more regulation or not, the old system is well and truly dead. Who will believe a rating agency when it puts an AAA rating on a securitized product ever again? The crash has solved that problem.

The Crisis Goes On and On and On

The crisis came, it did not end, and the debate started. How bad is the crisis? Will it spread? Is this purely a financial crisis, or will it adversely affect the broader economy? What should the central banks do? Should they continue to provide the market with liquidity? Reduce prime lending rates? This was a particularly hot topic among central bankers.

The U.S. real estate market continued to deteriorate in August and September 2007. Financial economist Robert J. Shiller of Yale University, the coauthor of the Case-Shiller Home Price Index, predicted that parts of the United States could expect to see declines in value of up to 50 percent to bring mortgages back in line with rents. Shiller's opinion was not well-received as the general consensus was that the decline in prices would soon be over.

The story took its most dramatic turn in the United Kingdom, where Northern Rock, a mortgage bank, became subject to a classic bank run, after the BBC announced that the bank was in financial difficulty on the morning of September 14, 2007. Customers stood in long lines to close their accounts with Northern Rock. Online customers complained that they could not log into their accounts, because Northern Rock's computer systems were hopelessly overloaded. Within two days, customers had withdrawn £ 2 billion from their Northern Rock accounts. The crisis was resolved by an impromptu bailout.

The second important event was the fall meeting of the International Monetary Fund (IMF) in Washington, D.C., at which the credit crisis, naturally, was the main topic. The hope was that the talks and the meeting of finance ministers of the seven biggest industrialized nations would shed some light on the problem. The attendees at the G-7 meeting agreed to ask the financial stability forum—a group of central bankers and regulators headed by Italian Central Bank President Mario Draghi—to draw up a set of recommendations for the future. The central banks, of course, sought to assign blame to market players instead of themselves, resulting in a relatively lukewarm list of recommendations. One recommendation was to increase transparency and examine the role of hedge funds more closely. Of course, no one hit upon the idea that the crisis could have had something to do with the central banks' low interest rate policies, or with the functioning of the banking system, which was, after all, well regulated.

A senior banker hit the nail on the head when he said, at the end of the meeting, that he had been more optimistic when flying to Washington, D.C., than when returning home. By that time, it was clear to everyone involved that the crisis was not over by a long shot. It was at this time that people started to realize that they were dealing with something else other than an ordinary banking crisis.

The IMF also warned of the long-term ramifications of this crisis. To the majority of observers, the worst seemed to be over in October. We are still talking 2007! At least the banks thought they had an idea of the losses that had been incurred. And yet no one knew what would happen next. This sense of insecurity dominated the mood at the IMF meeting. In particular, the attendees were concerned about how the crisis would affect the world economy. The U.S. economy was already beginning to decline at this point. The plunge in house prices seemed to be accelerating, and it was also unclear whether and how a slowing U.S. economy or even a recession would affect the rest of the world economy.

In early November, when some imagined that the crisis was already over, problems arose in another part of the credit market that seemed even more obscure. So-called "monoline insurers," that is, financial firms that specialized in insuring bond issues, especially American municipal bonds, or "munis," were suddenly in deep trouble. On November 1, there was a mini-crash among financial stocks.

There was a recovery in December, and it was typical for those months, that periods of acute crisis and periods of recovery in the stock market followed upon each other. A good indicator of this wave-shaped nature of the crisis is known as the TED Spread. The word *spread* refers to the difference between two interest rates. As shown in Figure 2.1, the TED Spread measures the difference between the interest rate for three-month U.S. Treasury bills, considered among the safest securities in the world, and the three-month interest rate in the

Figure 2.1 TED Spread. The difference, in percent, between the market rate on three-month Treasury bills and three-month LIBOR.

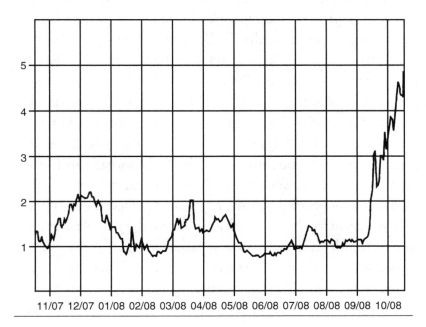

11/07 12/07 01/08 02/08 03/08 04/08 05/08 06/08 07/08 08/08 09/08 10/08

money markets. Normally the two rates should not differ by very much. In the money market, banks lend money to each other with no collateral whatsoever. In the past, when banks trusted one another, the interbank lending rate was the lowest in the market, not unlike the interest rates for government bonds. But a wide gap had developed between the two rates since the crisis erupted in August 2007. This was because the banks lost confidence in one another or, as economist Paul De Grauwe wrote, the banks lost confidence in the system as a whole. A year later, the problem was no longer that it was hard to tell whether a given bank was insolvent, but that the market assumed that large parts of the entire banking system were insolvent.

To return to the earthquake metaphor: The TED Spread was a good seismograph for the crisis. The bigger this interest rate spread, the greater was the lack of confidence among banks. As the graph indicates, the TED Spread went up in December 2007, again in March 2008, and finally, jumped sharply in September–October 2008. The money market was completely dry in October 2008. There was demand, but no supply. At the time, the TED Spread rose to well above 4 percent. Normally, the TED Spread is a small number slightly above zero. Throughout the entire crisis, the TED Spread hardly ever dipped below 1 percent, and it always rose sharply during the biggest moments of the crisis, beginning in December 2007.

The reason for the first increase was that the year was coming to a close, which meant that companies and banks were about to prepare their annual financial statements. There had been considerable turbulence in the money markets in November. The banks wanted to ensure that they would have sufficient cash available at the end of the year to settle potential outstanding claims. This led to considerable demand in late November for one-month funds, that is, loans in the interbank market with terms of one month. Because the crisis was still underway at this time, the banks had to adjust their balance sheets accordingly. Meanwhile, many of the SPVs had been reintegrated into the banks' balance sheets. Some of the asset-backed securities, the market for which had almost completely collapsed, had to be written off. It was completely unclear as to how these write-downs were to be handled and how much should be written off. There was a great deal of uncertainty, which prompted banks to secure adequate cash to be prepared for surprises. The situation continued to deteriorate during the course of December, and the TED Spread increased to above 2 percent.

The Central Banks Turn on the Printing Presses

The central banks reacted to this situation. The Federal Reserve was among the most proactive central banks. After it reduced the Fed Funds Target rate from 5.25 to 4.75 percent in September 2007, there were two additional rate cuts, in October and December, which brought the prime rate down to 4.25 percent. At that point, however, the U.S. rates were still slightly higher than the European short-term rates. That was soon about to change.

The Fed's most important decision, in December, was to substantially increase the liquidity supply. The Fed operates through so-called "open market operations" in the Fed Funds market, using a network of roughly 20 preferred money market dealers. As we have already discussed, the Fed buys and sells securities from banks, crediting or debiting banks' reserve accounts. If the Fed buys securities, it credits the banks' reserve accounts, and there creates, or prints, money.

In Europe, the system works a little differently through a mechanism known as securities repurchase operations, also known as repos. With repos, the European Central Bank (ECB) gives credits to banks in exchange for securities as collateral. Two weeks later the operation is reversed. The bank pays back the loan, plus interest rates (at the repo), and they get their collateral back.

On December 12, 2007, the Fed decided to introduce a so-called "Term Auction Facility," or TAF. A TAF is a repo auction that enables all 7,000 American banks to gain direct access to the Fed. The funds are essentially one-month funds or, to be more precise, central bank loans with a term of up to 35 days. For the Fed, the introduction of the TAF was a true revolution. In addition, the Fed and the ECB agreed to provide each other with money, using a foreign exchange swap. The idea was to give European banks access to dollar liquidity. They had a lot of dollar exposures.

As the TED Spread graph shows, the situation calmed down at the beginning of the year. At the end of January, the Fed reduced the Fed Funds Target rate by 0.75 percent, to 3.5 percent, and a few days later reduced it again, this time to 3 percent. Then, in March, it went down to 2.25 percent and in April to 2 percent. It remained there until early October, when it was cut by another 0.5 percent.

The ECB was slower than the Fed. In fact, it even raised interest rates during that period, from 4 to 4.25 percent for a short time in July, because of the sharp rise in inflation in the spring and summer. By this time, the oil price had jumped to a record high of $140 per barrel, and the ECB wanted to prevent higher commodities prices from leading to elevated inflation expectations.

The Bear Comes

The mood was still relatively optimistic in early March 2008. Of course the crisis had not ended yet. American real estate prices were still in free fall, and most experts agreed that the crisis would not end until real estate prices had reached a bottom because it was impossible to determine the value of a securitized subprime product as long as the market was in decline. But at least a systematic bank crisis did not develop. At this time, there were also optimists who felt that none of this was overly disconcerting. We eschew the satisfaction of naming these observers here. The International Monetary Fund made headlines with its assessment that the banks would have to write off up to $1 trillion. It was the highest estimate yet, shocking to many, and since then it has been revised upward considerably. But in early March 2008, it still looked as though the banking system would be able to cope with the crisis, although it would certainly impose a considerable burden on banks.

This assessment would change radically by the middle of the month.

During the week of March 10, 2008, there were rumors that the New York investment bank Bear Stearns was insolvent. It is very difficult to prove today whether and to what extent these rumors were true at the time. At any rate, the investment bank spent an entire week trying to discount the rumors. Bear Stearns was one of the most aggressive investment banks during the subprime boom, and there were fears that it could face extremely high write-down losses. No one knew exactly how high these losses would be, but as is so often the case in these situations, all it takes to drive a bank into the abyss is a rumor coupled with a deep-seated sense of anxiety. Bear Stearns, as its CEO Alan Schwartz later said, experienced a classic bank run.

Bear Stearns was not a standard bank with customers who had their checking or savings accounts there. For an investment bank, a bank run means that other banks are refusing to provide it with additional liquidity. Bear Stearns was suddenly no longer able to refinance itself, because banks were afraid that it would be unable to pay back a loan. In light of later events, this concern was not exactly irrational. As Mervyn King, the governor of the Bank of England, once said: "Once a run has begun, it was completely rational for people to want to participate in it. The only irrational thing about it is the way it begins, and there are even rational reasons for that." Bear Stearns barely managed to survive until the weekend, in a week marked by talks with the Federal Reserve and other parties. The content of these discussions was not known to the public at the time. Even the New York newspapers did not smell trouble brewing, nor did they anticipate the final outcome of the meetings.

On the evening of Sunday, March 16, the Federal Reserve released the shocking news that another bank, JP Morgan Chase, had acquired the investment bank Bear Stearns for the very low price of $2 per share. It was about one-tenth the share price on the previous Friday, which was already significantly lower than it had been earlier in the week. In addition, the Fed issued a nonrecourse loan to JP Morgan Chase for $30, assuming the risk of some of Bear Stearns's assets.

It was the biggest bailout since the rescue of the hedge fund Long-Term Capital Management in 1998. The difference, this time, was that the Fed was playing an active role. It was a classic bailout. Fed Chairman Ben Bernanke and his colleagues described the bailout of Bear Stearns as a necessary evil. Even though Bear Stearns itself was not a bank, the collapse of a bank that size would have had devastating consequences for the financial system as a whole. Bear Stearns was one of the biggest players in the market for credit default swaps (CDSs). Bear Stearns was one of the largest writers of CDS insurance. If it had been allowed to go bankrupt, many of those contracts would have become worthless, and this would have had ripple effects on the rest of the global financial system. Of course, no one knows exactly what would have happened if the Fed had not bailed out Bear Stearns. But that was precisely what the Fed did a few months later, just with another investment bank, when it allowed Lehman Brothers to fail. The decision triggered a dramatic crash.

The Bear Stearns bailout was a major shock to the system, but it also had a calming effect, because it showed that the government (whose consent the Fed needed to take action) was prepared to play the part of the white knight. Testifying before the U.S. Congress sometime later, Bernanke said that the Bear Stearns bailout prevented the likelihood of a collapse of the entire system, and that he no longer believed that this would occur.

Bernanke was wrong.

Fannie, Freddie, Lehman, AIG

Neither Fannie Mae nor Freddie Mac was a direct player in the subprime crisis itself. But they too played an important role in the mortgage market as a whole. They too relaxed the market's formerly high standards, if only in one segment. And that segment also crashed. The entire market was affected. In early July, the crisis hit Fannie and Freddie, which resulted in acute insolvency. The former chief executive of the Federal Reserve Bank of St. Louis, William Poole, described Fannie Mae as "technically insolvent." Fannie and Freddie, like so many other members of the so-called shadow banking system, operated with a capital base that was much too small. They borrowed money on a grand scale and used the funds to develop increasingly bizarre products, for which there were suddenly no longer any buyers. When the market collapsed, their game was over. The air had become too thin for these companies. The problem was not even a short-term lack of liquidity, which could have been resolved quickly. Fannie and Freddie were truly insolvent, as Poole said. In other words, the sum of their debts was higher than the sum of their assets, which had already been merged by then. In the week leading up to Friday, July 11, the Fannie Mae share price plummeted. As with Bear Stearns a few months earlier, the mortgage giants managed to survive until the weekend, at which point the U.S. government announced that it would do everything it could to keep Fannie and Freddie afloat. It was an explicit guarantee, in contrast to the implicit guarantee offered by the title "government-sponsored" that had reassured the market in the past.

The situation became somewhat less tense during the summer vacation months. The two significant events in this period were the slide in the price of oil and the surprising rise of the dollar. At this time, the markets seemed to recognize that the situation in Europe was hardly any better than in the United States, which led to a reassessment. The indicators of the general mood, especially in Europe, showed very clearly that the economy was in decline. But none of this was a reflection of a special crisis, but rather a perfectly normal cyclical development. The crisis was still simmering, but a certain sense of normalcy prevailed.

Many believed that the acute phase of the financial crisis was over, despite ongoing problems. But the real problem would have been a recession. As had happened so often in the past, the severe dynamics of this crisis were underestimated. It reached its peak in the months of September and October 2008.

The government bailout of Fannie and Freddie marked the beginning of this development. On September 7, the U.S. government officially seized control of the two mortgage giants, placing them under the conservatorship of the Federal Housing Finance Agency, a move that former Treasury Secretary Hank Paulson had stipulated as a condition of releasing taxpayer money. The total losses suffered by Fannie and Freddie at the time amounted to $14.9 billion. The U.S. government promised a financial injection totaling $200 billion in the form of loans and fresh capital. Fannie and Freddie held securities and loans worth $5 trillion, or about half the annual gross domestic product (GDP) of the United States. An undefined portion of this total was acutely threatened by the mortgage crisis. It was the first significant takeover of financial institutions by the government during this crisis.

But many commentators were still skeptical, even in the days after September 7. They were convinced that the peak of the crisis must have been reached already. After Bear Stearns, Fannie and Freddie, the last two major risks had been set aside.

This optimism would also prove to be misguided within only a few days. In fact, many dangers still existed. The quasi-insurance market of credit default swaps (CDSs) was still a ticking time bomb. Far too little was known about the financial condition of the so-called shadow banking market, that is, financial players that were not official banks and yet conducted bank-like transactions, such as investment banks and hedge funds. At the time, however, the risk of a total collapse of the global financial system still existed. The problem was that although it was known that the risk was not trivial, it still could not be quantified. Even the central bankers, who normally have access to somewhat better information than journalists, were helpless.

Despite the Fannie and Freddie bailout, the crisis came to a head once again in the week of September 8–14. At that point, Lehman Brothers, Goldman Sachs, Morgan Stanley, and Merrill Lynch were still the four main, independent investment banks left standing. Bear Stearns had been the fifth, but now it was part of a larger banking group. The investment banks were the main players in the financial crisis, the kings of the largely unregulated shadow banking market and the principal engineers of products in the credit market. Indeed, they were the most important connection to hedge funds, and Lehman was one of the most important among them.

The head of Lehman Brothers for many years was Richard Fuld, one of Wall Street's former "masters of the universe." Between 2000 and 2008, Fuld earned a whopping $484.8 million, close to half a billion dollars. Of course, Fuld did not repay the money after the Lehman bankruptcy. Instead, he said that the pain of the Lehman bankruptcy would stay with him for the rest of his life. And so did the money.

One of the fundamental problems of investment banks—and of many standard banks, too—was that they had too little capital relative to the risks they carried. They held their assets in the form of questionable securities, for which there had not been a liquid market for more than a year. More and more write-downs were necessary, and the capital base became smaller and smaller. Initially, these firms, including Lehman, tried to raise additional capital.

The first attempt, in early September 2008, was the establishment of a so-called "bad bank." The idea was to separate the good and bad parts of a bank. As a result, the good bank became more creditworthy and solvent and the bad bank was managed separately, the goal being to sell the questionable products or turn a profit with them at a later point. The idea of a bad bank sounds like an attempt to overcome gravity. It was typical of the way bankers' minds worked during the waning period of the credit boom. Just as they had once thought they could magically transform bad loans into good securities, they now believed that they could turn a bad bank into a good one by simply building a fence around the good part and lumping together the bad.

But what may have worked in 2007 was no longer possible in 2008. The market had lost too much confidence. At this point, Lehman was already in talks with the Korea Development Bank, which wanted to inject $6 billion in new capital into the "good bank." With the money, Lehman planned to finance the bad bank. It wanted the bad bank to have $8 billion in total capital resources, plus an additional $24 billion in loans.

The Koreans were not enthusiastic about this good bank/bad bank idea. They would have preferred to participate in a normal capital expansion, but at a low price. In the end, the transaction failed because of opposition from the South Korean government. On Monday, September 8, the future of Lehman Brothers was hanging by a thread.

On September 9, the well-known U.S. economist Kenneth Rogoff, a former chief economist at the International Monetary Fund and now a professor at Harvard University, published an article in which he warned central banks against overly generous financial injections. Rogoff argued that the financial system had to shrink, and that not every bank could be saved. A credit risk, he wrote, could easily turn into a sovereign risk.

Rogoff was not the only critic. The Federal Reserve was under considerable pressure not to save all banks that came to it for help. This pressure was greater in September than it had been in the past, and it was certainly Lehman Brothers' bad luck to have gotten itself into difficulties at this particular time. The general belief, at the time, was that Hank Paulson could not afford to rescue another major investment bank, after Bear Stearns, Fannie and Freddie. Besides, Lehman did not play as big a role in the U.S. real estate market.

This proved to be a giant misjudgment.

On September 11, Lehman's share price plunged after very poor quarterly numbers were released, which revealed that the bank had lost $3.9 billion after taking write-downs of $5.6 billion. When the news came out that the rating agencies planned to downgrade Lehman stock, the share price fell by 46 percent in a single day. This brought the decline in the Lehman share price to 89 percent over the last 12 months. At that point, it was clear that the bank no longer had a future as an independent institution, and that only a day or two remained to sell the bank. The weekend of September 13–14 would become the most important weekend since the crisis began.

The press was naming various banks as potential buyers of Lehman: competitor Goldman Sachs, Bank of America, JC Flowers, and even the Chinese Investment Company. Hank Paulson met with the Federal Reserve in an attempt to put together a rescue package for Lehman Brothers.

At the same time, another piece of news was causing turmoil elsewhere on Wall Street. The stock price of the insurance giant American International Group (AIG) suddenly plunged by 30 percent. AIG is the world's second-largest insurance company, after Germany's Allianz. But unlike Allianz, AIG was also one of the main players in the credit markets, where it operated as an insurer in the market for credit default swaps (CDSs) mentioned earlier. The failure of AIG would have meant the total collapse of this market and, with it, the total collapse of the global financial system.

AIG was an American institution. Founded in 1919, AIG developed into the leading insurance company in the United States and later in the world. Cornelius Vander Starr founded the company at the age of 27. In the 1960s, he turned over control to Maurice "Hank" Greenberg, whose name is now inseparably linked to AIG. Greenberg modernized and expanded AIG with great success. In 2005, following an accounting scandal, AIG paid a fine of $1.6 billion, which led to Greenberg's ouster. But the company's problems grew even further after his departure. Risk management was neglected. AIG increasingly invested in the CDS business, which, though lucrative in the short term, was also highly risky. Those risks became even greater, and although there had been no collapse of a major bank yet, AIG was faced with substantial losses. In September 2008, the risks suddenly seemed to be much higher than they had been only a year earlier. AIG made a classic mistake for an insurance company, namely to systematically underestimate the total risk.

On Saturday, September 13, it was revealed that AIG wanted to sell $20 billion in assets to improve its financial position. It would not be the last time that AIG had to go, cap in hand, to the government. Nor was it the last time that AIG hit television's top stories and newspaper headlines.

On September 13, the market still believed that Lehman Brothers would be sold and that AIG would save itself by selling assets.

Over the weekend Britain's Barclays Bank had emerged as a possible buyer of Lehman Brothers, but then Barclays withdrew from the negotiations. Without assurances from the U.S. government or the participation of other banks, the British bank was unwilling to assume the risk on its own. The British prime minister, Gordon Brown, took the ultimate decision not to provide any guarantees to Barclays, which in turn sealed the fate of that takeover.

On Monday morning, without a bailout or direct aid from the federal government or the Federal Reserve, Lehman had no other choice but to declare bankruptcy. The news became increasingly grim after that, with the headlines filled with even more shocking news. Bank of America had acquired the investment bank Merrill Lynch for $44 billion. At the same time, the U.S. government was still trying to save AIG, where the situation was becoming more and more dramatic. AIG announced that it was seeking an immediate infusion of capital, and it eventually asked the Federal Reserve for a stopgap loan numbering in the billions. At the same time, there were rumors of the possible insolvency of a large American savings and loan bank, Washington Mutual. AIG received the approval to tap $20 billion of its subsidiaries' capital, but that didn't help much. The rating agencies threatened to downgrade its stock, which the company would not survive.

There was no solution for Lehman Brothers, which filed for Chapter 11 bankruptcy that Monday. At the Lehman Brothers Building in the Docklands district of East London, hundreds of employees cleared their desks, packed their personal belongings into boxes, and left the bank. A similar scene unfolded in New York, where tourists hurried to the bank's headquarters to photograph its devastated employees as they left the building.

That Monday also brought the downgrading of AIG. At first, there were fears that AIG would have to deposit more collateral for its CDS contracts. This is because CDSs are derivatives that are based on an underlying payment obligation. To ensure that the issuer can live up to this payment obligation if a credit event occurs, the insurers deposit collateral, the amount of which is based on their own ratings. The higher the rating, the lower the required collateral deposit. This also means that a downgrade can quickly turn into a disaster, or a sort of self-fulfilling prophecy. On the morning of Monday, September 15, AIG barely managed to avert this vicious circle. Nevertheless, it still needed $14 billion in immediate liquidity.

Four monumental events had occurred on a single weekend. Lehman Brothers, one of the world's most prestigious investment banks, was bankrupt. Merrill Lynch had been sold off. AIG, America's largest insurance company, was on the verge of bankruptcy, as was Washington Mutual, one of the country's biggest banks. The meltdown of the global financial system had begun.

Then came yet another big surprise: The U.S. government, which only hours earlier had refused to rescue Lehman Brothers, was suddenly willing to rescue AIG. The $85 billion cash infusion at AIG was practically the equivalent of a nationalization of the insurance group. The U.S. government calculated that an AIG bankruptcy would trigger a systematic crisis in the entire financial system. It also calculated that Lehman Brothers was not as important to the system. Big mistake. But this is easier to say with hindsight, than it was at the time.

The Near Meltdown of the Global Financial System

As we have already mentioned, the TED Spread was considered the most reliable seismograph of the crisis. It shot upward in the first few weeks of September. Even the AIG bailout and the news of the Federal Reserve's plans to inject additional liquidity into the economy did not impress the markets. The TED Spread reached a value of 2.83 percent, a peak at the time, but things were about to deteriorate even further.

Federal Reserve Chairman Ben Bernanke was quoted as saying: "We have lost control." As honest as this statement was, it didn't exactly help calm the markets. During the course of the week, with the money market drying up rapidly, the Fed, the European Central Bank, and the Bank of Japan pumped close to a quarter billion dollars into the market.

The wave of nationalizations was accompanied by the first regulatory changes. The Americans led the way by issuing a temporary ban on short sales. A short sale is the sale of securities by someone who doesn't own the securities, but is then required to purchase them at a later date. Short selling is a strategy used by someone who speculates that the price of a given security will fall. The banks suspected speculators of forcing their share prices down with short-selling attacks.

At the end of the week, former U.S. Federal Reserve Chairman Paul Volcker wrote that it was time to resurrect the Resolution Trust Corporation (RTC), a government-run asset management company that bought up banks, liquidated the assets, and later privatized them again. The RTC was created in the late 1980s to solve the crisis in the American savings and loan industry, in which many institutions had made reckless investments during the pre-1987 boom.

By the end of the week in mid-September, the first rumors began circulating that then Treasury Secretary Hank Paulson was working on a big plan. The details were released by the weekend. Under the plan, the U.S. Treasury would spend $700 billion to revive the market for asset-backed securities (ABSs). The idea was that the government would buy the securities from the banks at inflated prices, so as to overcome the valuation crisis. The reaction from economists was unusually unanimous and negative. Almost all economists who commented on the subject criticized Paulson's plan and called it fundamentally wrong. Their central argument was that the plan did not solve the problem of a structurally undercapitalized banking sector. What the economy needed was a series of injections of new capital. The Paulson plan only recapitalized the banks indirectly by somewhat sweetening their toxic securities.

Paulson also wanted there to be no oversight over how the $700 billion was to be spent. The plan even stipulated that decisions made by the Treasury Secretary could "not be reviewed by any court of law." Paulson's plan encountered almost total opposition in Congress. The Democrats felt that it was too unfair, because taxpayers were taking on all of the risk without being given the chance to benefit from the fruits of the bailout in the future. For many market fundamentalist Republicans, the plan was an excessively deep intervention into the free market. Fed Chairman Bernanke begged the Congress not to sabotage the plan, arguing that not passing the legislation could trigger a depression.

Negotiations at the White House in the ensuing days led to some aspects of the plan being modified. The new version gave Congress oversight over the Treasury's actions and the government the opportunity to take stakes in the banks. During a critical moment in the negotiations, as the *New York Times* reported, Paulson fell to his knees before Nancy Pelosi, the Democratic speaker of the House of Representatives, and begged her not to jeopardize the plan. She told him that the problem was not the Democrats in Congress but the Republicans. At the same time, the number of critics of the Paulson plan began to grow. Richard Fisher, the president of the Federal Reserve Bank of Dallas, publicly expressed doubts as to the effectiveness of the bailout plan, because it would significantly increase government debt. But by the weekend, it appeared that the White House and Congress had agreed to a compromise—the Troubled Asset Relief Program, or TARP. Meanwhile, JP Morgan Chase had bought up what was left of Washington Mutual, but hardly anyone was interested anymore.

In Berlin, German Finance Minister Peer Steinbrück, brimming with self-righteousness, felt the need to explain to the German parliament, the Bundestag, that U.S. dominance as an economic superpower was over. The financial crisis, he said, was primarily an American matter. That, too, proved to be a tremendous error of judgment.

The crisis reached Europe shortly after Steinbrück's ill-spoken words. During that week, the share price of the Belgian-Dutch Fortis Bank fell dramatically. The reason was all too familiar. A value adjustment had resulted in an insufficient capital base, and the bank urgently needed new capital. Because this triggered growing fears of insolvency among other banks, a bank like Fortis had great difficulties obtaining the necessary liquidity in the short term. By the end of the week, Fortis was on the brink of bankruptcy. Over the weekend, cabinet ministers from Belgium, the Netherlands, and Luxembourg met to assemble a bailout package for Fortis. A total of €11.2 billion in new capital was injected into the bank, and suddenly the Belgian government owned 49 percent of Fortis. The shareholders later unraveled the deal, and the Belgian prime minister was forced to resign. An accord subsequently emerged many months later. The episode was a good example of the mess involved with resolving cross-border European banks. Everyone and no one was responsible.

On that weekend, French President Nicolas Sarkozy convened a meeting with German Chancellor Angela Merkel, Italian Prime Minister Silvio Berlusconi, and British Prime Minister Gordon Brown to discuss the situation. The Dutch had previously proposed a European version of the TARP worth €300 billion. The French finance minister also voiced her support of the plan. But Merkel and her finance minister rejected the idea before it could even be discussed. "Everyone should sort his own shit out," Sarkozy quoted Merkel as saying, according to the generally well-informed French satirical newspaper *Le Canard Enchaîné*. When Sarkozy learned of Germany's resistance, he distanced himself from the plan, but he was snubbed by Merkel.

Germany was adamantly opposed to a European solution. As Steinbrück later said, the Germans wanted to retain control over their own affairs. At this point, however, who believes that politicians are still in control of this process?

The summit ended on a sour note. Germany blocked France's efforts to develop a general European plan, and the parties agreed that it would be up to each country to rescue its own banking system. By that point, it was clear that a European solution was not to be expected from Merkel and Sarkozy or their respective finance ministers. The Italians also favored a European plan, but they too were unable to prevail. The politicians had failed, and by then even the markets no longer had any confidence in the U.S. plan.

The markets' revenge came in the week that began on Monday, October 6. When viewed across the entire week, it was either the biggest or the second-biggest market crash of all times, even worse than the crashes of 1929 and 1987. There was only one other week, in 1933, which saw bigger price declines on markets in the United States. First the Dow Jones fell below 10,000, then it plunged to below 8,000, and finally it stabilized at 8,500. The DAX, the German stock index, plunged initially to below 6,000, then went down to less than 5,000 and ended the week at slightly above 4,500. Irrespective of the region or segment of the economy, it was a global and systematic market crash. The TED Spread shot up to previously unheard-of levels, reaching 4.6 percent by the end of the week. It is no exaggeration to say that the money market no longer existed at that point.

During that chaotic week, there was also a coordinated reduction in interest rates by the major central banks. But it too was no longer effective. Without a money market, interest rates are practically irrelevant for the real economy. Rates for short-term loans depend on interest rates in the money markets, rates with names like LIBOR and EURIBOR. These rates were hardly affected by the change in the base or prime rates. In addition, the European Central Bank decided to make an unlimited amount of cash available through the repo market. Banks were to receive as much money as they wanted, available at the attractive repo rate. They were no longer required to bid, but merely had to deposit the necessary collateral.

There were those who argued that the extremely strong liquidity policies of the central banks only exacerbated the situation in the money markets. Because the banks were getting all of their liquidity from the central banks, they no longer needed to rely on the money markets for their short-term borrowing.

In addition to the supply disappearing because the banks had lost confidence in each other, demand suddenly fell. Of course, this raised the question: Under these circumstances, how does one get the market back into motion?

There were others who argued that a money market was no longer needed, and that the central banks could perform most of its functions. The only problem with this approach is that the machinery of our monetary economy is completely dependent on the money markets. In Spain, almost every citizen is familiar with the three-month EURIBOR money market rate, because it serves as the basis for almost every mortgage. The same applies to Italy, where a one-month EURIBOR is the key interest rate for mortgages. A different situation applies in Germany, where mortgages are heavily collateralized through the capital market. Germany has a different system. But many corporate loans are also based on the LIBOR or EURIBOR. Under these conditions, a central bank can pump as much cheap money into the banking system as it wishes, but as long as the money market is defunct, an interest rate reduction will have no effect on the real economy.

Iceland Melts Down

This was a global economic crisis, and while it originated in the United States, America was not the country worst hit by this crisis. Without a doubt, the country that faired the poorest was Iceland.

This small island in the North Atlantic has a mere 300,000 residents, the size of a medium-sized American or European city. But before the crisis struck, Iceland was one of the richest countries in the world, with a per capita income of $54,000 per head of population.

Before all this happened Iceland was a country of fishermen and farmers. It developed some manufacturing niches in the twentieth century, but this was not what produced the big money for the country. What really made money was the banking system, which was deregulated in 2001. Iceland became one of the major players in our modern transaction-based capitalism, with its three major banks, Kaupthing, Landsbanki, and Glitnir. Essentially, the country turned into a giant, super-leveraged hedge fund. The banks operated mainly abroad, in Europe especially, where Icelandic banks offered the most attractive deposit interest rates available on the market. Naïve German savers and British municipal authorities all invested in the domestic subsidiaries of Icelandic banks. Those subsidiaries were not covered by the national deposit insurance schemes, which proved to be a big problem later on. A bank cannot offer persistently higher deposit rates than the rest of the market without incurring some severe risks. And this is exactly what happened here. Icelandic banks were among the biggest gamblers in global credit markets

The trouble was that these banks were rather large compared to the size of their home country. As a result, they were too large to be bailed out. The assets of the bank system were more than ten times as large as the country's annual economic output. And many other alarm bells had started ringing in the years before the crisis. The current account was broadly balanced during the 1990s, but in the late 1990s it started to increase, with a short interruption, to a level of some 25 percent in 2005. The current account deficit is essentially the trade deficit, plus or minus financial transfers (people sending money back to their home, profits being repatriated in and out). The U.S. economy had a current account deficit of almost 7 percent of GDP in the year 2007, a level which was considered unsustainable. While there is no single number that separates sustainable or unsustainable current account deficits for every country—it depends on the types of financial flows, the stage of the country's development, and many other factors—a current account deficit in the order of 25 percent of GDP is definitely beyond the pale under any circumstance, and potentially very dangerous. Iceland was the classic example of a country that was living far beyond its means and was so blinded by the boom that it perceived its newfound wealth as something of a reward for hard work.

Even more worrying than the current account deficit was the country's international investment position, which reached a whopping negative 125 percent of GDP in 2006. This is the difference between investments you have abroad and investments foreigners have in your country. It was the worst performance of all countries in the Organisation for Economic Co-operation and Development (OECD). But the worst indicator of all was Iceland's indebtedness. While households and government debts remained reasonably contained, the debt levels of the nonfinancial corporations in Iceland jumped from a little over 50 percent of GDP to almost 300 percent.

As everywhere else, the Icelandic banks also gambled with relatively little bank capital and raked in enormous profits. Most of that money was made—guess where—in the real estate sector. By the time the global crisis arrived, Iceland had already made some first efforts to reduce these substantial imbalances.

Nevertheless, it was too late, as the financial markets globally began to panic about the state of the banks, particularly Icelandic banks. A number of speculative attacks on the small country occurred throughout 2008, putting enormous pressure on its currency, the Icelandic krona. The central bank reacted by raising its key interest rate to 15 percent, hoping to stop the speculation. But all this made the Icelandic banks' predicament even worse, and so a self-fulfilling crisis started to emerge, when Iceland's banks were no longer in a position to roll over their debts. Iceland's banks worked like the aforementioned SIV. They borrowed short-term funds on the money market, and used the money to place highly leveraged bets. When the money market froze up, it was "game over" for Iceland's banks. The country's central bank was too small to act as a lender of last resort. Iceland's banks were bigger than the country itself. There was no safety net.

The total amount of debt by Iceland's three largest banks had been estimated at €50 billion, or about €170,000 per Icelandic resident, nine times as large as the country's GDP. When the global money market froze up completely in September, Iceland's crisis started in earnest. In late September, Glitnir Bank was on the verge of bankruptcy. The government stepped in and nationalized the bank. The following week, it took control of Landsbanki. The following week it nationalized the country's largest bank, Kaupthing. The Icelandic government thought that nationalizing the banking system was the right course of action. The prime minister said the country would have otherwise faced a total economic collapse. But even with the nationalization of the banking sector, the economy was headed for a serious depression.

Given the foreign exposure of Icelandic banks, more than half a million depositors had their bank accounts frozen. This included German banks, and many individual savers, since the Icelandic banks advertised their high deposit heavily in the European financial press. British municipalities had more than €1 billion invested in Icelandic banks, and Prime Minister Brown even invoked the country's anti-terrorism laws to freeze Icelandic assets in Great Britain. In early October, Iceland faced not only the imminent collapse of its banking system, but, despite what its prime minister was saying, also a collapse of the entire economy similar to what Argentina had experienced at the beginning of the decade.

To get out of its temporary mess, Iceland was in urgent need of bridging finance to roll over the country's debt. The government had held exploratory talks with Russia over a $4 billion loan, which made many European countries very nervous. On October 24, the government reached a deal with the IMF on a bridging loan, but this was later stopped by the United Kingdom and Holland, as the disputes over compensation of savers had not yet been settled. A final IMF-led package of $4.6 billion was finally agreed upon on November 19. Almost half of that money came from the IMF, the balance from an assorted collection of Scandinavian countries. Germany, the Netherlands, and the United Kingdom also chipped in.

Iceland has since become a symbol of the hazards emanating from this banking crisis. During those turbulent days in the end September and into early October, the Icelandic stock market effectively melted down. It lost 90 percent of its value.

Iceland was an example of a most speculator case of how the crisis destroyed a country's economy. The crisis also had devastating effects in many emerging markets. In central and eastern Europe, several countries also ran Iceland-style current account deficits, such as the Ukraine and Latvia. We have also seen a run on the currencies in these regions as well. In Hungary, which suffered relatively high twin deficits—budget and current account deficits—most households had their mortgages denominated in foreign currencies, mostly Swiss francs, because Swiss interest rates were much lower. Those countries obviously ran a higher risk that currency devaluation would drive those mortgage repayments sky-high, and this is exactly what happened in early 2009, when foreign investors got nervous and repatriated their investments. In Hungary, for example, almost the entire banking system was in the hands of foreign banks, mostly Austrian, so when the crisis struck, the foreigners ended the capital inflow, got their money out, and the Hungarians were stuck with a fast-depreciated exchange rate. The European Union provided a short-term balance of payment assistance, together with the IMF, but the central and eastern European countries were still not out of the water in late March 2009. The markets involved were mostly small and highly leveraged emerging markets. These countries had ignored the risk warnings that were there before the crisis, and they have paid a heavy price. Financial experts from several countries fear that the acute danger might persist for some time to come.

How to Rescue a Banking System

In the week during which the global stock markets crashed, the government in Berlin issued an unlimited guarantee for all private bank deposits and the British government nationalized eight banks, the finance ministers, and central bankers of the G-7 nations met in Washington, D.C.

In the last 20 years, these G-7 meetings and, later, G-8 meetings including Russia, have been relatively ineffective. In most cases, the participants reached their agreements ahead of the meeting, in the form of communiqués. By the time the world leaders actually came together, all of the decisions had already been made. The primary function of the politicians was to look impressive in the final group photo, thereby creating the impression that there was actually something called global cooperation. The politicians voiced their concerns about the problems of global warming, human rights, and Africa. But most of the times promises that were made were ignored, such as the promise to increase aid to the developing world.

On the evening of Friday, October 10, the G-7 finance ministers met in Washington, D.C., to discuss a bailout package. As was so often the case with these meetings, the politician's staffs fleshed out the communiqué in advance, and it contained the usual meaningless clichés. After all, no one wanted any surprises. The news that the G-7 ministers were simply sticking to the status quo, despite the extreme circumstances, came as yet another shock to the market.

The governments took the reaction of the markets and perhaps the criticisms of these economists very seriously. On the following Monday, October 13, 2008, the market was expected to plunge by another 20 percent. If this had happened, the meltdown of the global economic and financial system would have been complete. Within a few days, the global economy would have been in a shambles.

Even the Europeans moved. On Saturday, October 11, 2008, German Chancellor Merkel and French President Sarkozy met in Colombey-les-Deux-Églises, the hometown of Charles de Gaulle, the founder of the French Fifth Republic. In the wake of the previous weekend's disaster, the leaders were now determined to act together. Sarkozy convened a special summit meeting of the heads of state and government of the Eurozone. This group had never met before in this configuration. In the past, Germany had rejected any French initiative out of fear that the French planned to establish a European economic government as a counterweight to the European Central Bank. In this case, Merkel could do nothing but agree, or else the catastrophe would have been perfect.

The meetings of the heads of government produced the following agreement. First, the governments involved would offer a full guarantee, albeit for a limited time, of all debt issues by banks. This meant that the banks could borrow new capital for the medium term in the capital markets, and the governments would guarantee repayment of the loans for five years.

This applied to all 8,000 banks in the Eurozone. Second, banks would be recapitalized, because the capital cover was generally too low, particularly in Germany and Great Britain. Third, the plan called for changing accounting regulations so that banks and insurance companies could temporarily deviate from the mark-to-market accounting rule, which required banks to account for securities at market value. Without this change, many banks and insurance companies in Germany would have had to file for instant bankruptcy, because rapidly falling asset prices would have lowered the value of the banks' fixed assets far enough to make them insolvent.

The national plans were unveiled the next morning. Germany was providing a €500 billion package, of which €100 billion was available immediately for recapitalization and to cover the bank guarantees. Just as the banks once parked money in special purpose vehicles (SPVs), the federal government was now also conveniently keeping these sums off its own national balance sheet.

The plan announced in France that Monday was structured somewhat differently, but its economic impact was similar. Two government institutions were created to take on the task of recapitalizing the banks, on the one hand, and providing them with loans, on the other. The second institution was a sort of artificial money market. The government guarantee enabled the institution to borrow money cheaply, which it then lent to the banks at a markup. This gave banks access to short-term and medium-term loans, for which they could deposit somewhat shakey securities as collateral. Of course, the banks could also borrow as much as they wanted from the central bank, but only in return for depositing top-rated securities as collateral, such as government bonds. The fact that the banks were sitting on large numbers of toxic securities was behind the idea of allowing them to use these securities as collateral. Of course, this sort of thing only works with a government that is willing to accept losses.

The market reaction to this collection of bailout packages was euphoric. On Monday, October 13, most markets gained 10 percent, and the rally continued on Tuesday. But economists were reserved in their enthusiasm, arguing that the measures would prevent an immediate crisis but did not solve the entire problem. Other commentators were so confident that they even ventured to predict that the peak of the crisis had now been reached. This author was of a different opinion at the time.

On Wednesday, the release of unfavorable consumption figures caused markets in the United States to plunge once again, this time suffering the biggest single-day losses since 1987. The rally had been wiped out and the markets were back at the previous week's level. And money market rates, the barometer of this credit crisis, were on the rise once again.

So it was yet another bear rally end, another period of unjustified optimism. The bank rescue packages in Europe temporarily put the lid on the crisis, in the sense that finance ministers and central bankers did not have to save banks every weekend. But the packages did not help the situation.

In the United States, TARP was quickly considered a disaster. The financial and economic blogosphere, which was hugely influential during this crisis, derided this project as deeply flawed, essentially as fraud against the taxpayer, as it involved toxic securities, for which there was no market, at excessively high prices. It would not be a bailout of the shareholders in banks, but a genuine resource transfer from the taxpayers to the shareholders. The commentariat also criticized the way in which former Treasury Secretary Hank Paulson tried to exclude any Congressional and legal oversight over the process, so that he would have been able to spend the money as he saw fit, with no recourse to legal action. One assumed Paulson's position of nondisclosure was to ensure a degree of certainty among market participants, which is important especially in a financial crisis. But it backfired badly.

The U.S. administration made a number of changes to the program, the most important being a decision to buy preferred equity, which is a hybrid between ordinary stocks and bonds. Preferred shares have no ordinary voting rights, and they normally receive dividends, even when stockholders do not. The idea was not to dilute stockholders, which the Bush administration feared partly for ideological reasons and partly because of the stock market reaction. There was hope that preferred equity would nevertheless be considered as equity capital, rather than a loan; however, the critics saw it the other way around. Later the U.S. administration extended the program from mortgage-related products to consumer credit, and later again to anything they saw fit. When the Bush administration left office, around $400 billion of the $700 billion had been used up—and the situation of the banks had not improved.

When faced with a financial balance sheet crisis there are several different approaches available. Consideration must be given to a solution's total effectiveness, costs, and distribution of costs. Should the shareholders bear all the costs? Should the unsecured bondholders in the banks be asked to contribute? Should the taxpayers shoulder the burden? One of the criticisms of the TARP program was that it let the shareholders and bondholders off the hook.

TARP is part of what is generally known as a "bad bank" concept. The government sets up a bad bank, which buys up the assets for which the markets give no valuation at some price. The idea is that the uncertainty vanishes, and that it becomes quickly evident which bank needs new capital. Another idea is the "good bank," where the government sets up a bank that buys the good assets from the banks, then takes the banking license away from those banks and turns them into administrators of the bad assets. In this approach, the shareholders get clobbered.

Yet another approach is full-scale nationalization. The government would, by force, recapitalize the banks, thus diluting the existing shareholders. In the fall of 2008, the issue of nationalization was discussed mainly among experts. Governments at the time were clearly not ready for such radical action—which was very typical of the way they responded to the crisis. During that time, there was much interest in the Swedish experience, where nationalization was chosen after a severe financial crisis in the 1990s. The accompanying sidebar discusses in some detail how the Swedes did this.

What Happened in Sweden?

The following is a reprint of an article written by Lars Jonung, a policy advisor to the European Commission in Brussels.[1]

Banks all over the world are in deep trouble. This has created an interest in the successful bank resolution policy adopted in Sweden in the early 1990s. But can the Swedish model of yesterday be applied in other countries today?

When Sweden was hit by a financial crisis in 1991–93, its response comprised a unique combination of seven distinctive features: (1) swift policy action, (2) political unity, (3) a blanket government guarantee of all bank liabilities (including

(Continued)

---

[1] Published in Eurointelligence, March 6, 2009, http://www.eurointelligence .com/article.581+M5dabb199928.0.html

deposits but excluding shareholder capital), (4) an appropriate legal framework based on open-ended government funding, (5) complete information disclosure by banks asking for government support, (6) a differentiated resolution policy by which banks were classified according to their financial strength and treated accordingly, and (7) an overall monetary and fiscal policy that facilitated the bank resolution policy.

Two major banks were taken over by the government. Their assets were split into a good bank and a bad bank, the "toxic" assets of the latter being dealt with by asset-management companies (AMCs) which focused solely on the task of disposing of them. When transferring assets from the banks to the AMCs, cautious market values were applied, thus putting a floor under the valuation of such assets, mostly real estate. This restored demand and liquidity, and thus put a break on falling asset prices.

The Swedish model proved successful. The banking system was kept intact. It continued to function, swiftly emerged from the crisis and remained mainly in private hands. Taxpayers did not lose out in the long run. The net fiscal cost of the bank resolution 15 years after the crisis is close to zero. The policy priority of saving the banks, not the owners of the banks, kept moral hazard at bay.

The bank resolution policy was carried out transparently and openly. The center-right government under Carl Bildt cooperated with the social democratic opposition, creating public trust in the resolution process.

Today's global crisis is different from the Swedish crisis of the 1990s in important respects. The Swedish financial system was small, with only half a dozen major banks. It was also bank-based, with few major non-bank financial actors, and was less sophisticated and less globalized than the current world financial system.

Still, there are lessons from the Swedish resolution policy that may serve as guiding principles today.

First, the Swedish experience demonstrates that a genuine threat of public receivership or nationalization does galvanize banks into action. With this threat hanging over them, private banks in Sweden made great efforts to solve their problems themselves by asking their owners for capital. The lesson is that no government support should be given to a financial institution with zero or negative equity until its present owners have surrendered their control and ownership.

Banks and their networks of debtors and creditors should be saved—not bank owners and not bank managers. Once this principle is commonly accepted, government rescues will be easier to carry out. Moral hazard will be reined in—today

(Continued)

and in the future. Taxpayers will more readily accept the necessary public expenses.

Presently, policy choices are often hampered by a political dislike of public receivership (nationalization)—even if such a step would be economically more efficient and just. The Swedes, however, put ideology and fear of big government aside. Their priority, from the Conservative party to the Social Democrats, was to find a quick, workable solution.

Today, major steps towards pseudo-nationalization have been taken in many countries, creating the worst of all possible worlds: governments are financing bad banks without outright owning them and failed managers and owners are not punished. This creates public distrust in the resolution policy as a whole. Temporary public receivership with a clear exit strategy is a more efficient approach, and less costly to the taxpayers. As any student of finance knows, the value of a bankrupt bank is zero.

Second, the Swedish experience suggests that all banks that are put under public receivership should be split immediately into a good bank and a bad bank, under the control of an independent authority with the goal of terminating the operations of the bad bank in a specified time frame, say within less than 10 years. This avoids Japanese-style "zombie" banks. Alternative

solutions include purchase-and-assumption transactions, in which a part of a bank's good assets and
matching liabilities are sold to another bank.

The good bank should continue operation and
be re-privatized as soon as possible. The bad bank
should manage the bad assets taken from the old
bank with a view to selling them in due course.
This will help recreate a market for such assets.

Third, the Swedish case shows that the bank
resolution policy should have an open-ended
financial commitment from the government to be
credible and efficient. At this stage of the global
crisis, it is impossible to estimate exactly the cost of
rescuing a financial system in any country. However, the ad hoc measures that have been taken
in many countries seem to be an open invitation
for struggling banks and institutions to demand
more funds. Any attempt to fix a sum for the rescue
effort undermines its credibility. It should be made
clear that the government is ready to mobilize the
resources needed. Fighting a financial crisis is like
fighting a war. Losing is simply unthinkable.

Finally, the process of bank resolution should
be transparent, based on full disclosure of the steps
taken and the valuations of assets made. Openness
fosters public trust in the bank resolution policy
and in the financial system that will emerge after
the crisis. And trust is the basic building block of
any banking system.

Another important question related to the bondholders: Should they also be asked to contribute? Bonds issued by commercial banks enjoyed a reasonable yield spread over government bonds, so why should bondholders be treated with so much consideration? If you recapitalize, you only change the company's equity capital. Such an exercise should not affect the bondholders. They are only hit if the bank goes into liquidation—in which case they might lose everything. A way to avoid this is to apply what is known in the finance jargon as "a haircut." The bondholders would be protected, but they would suffer a symmetric loss, in the form of an agreed percentage on their holdings.

The reason to treat bondholders with some caution is financial stability. If you clobber the shareholders, you end up with 1,000 points or so down in the Dow Jones Industrial Average. But if you hit the bondholders, you are likely to end up with a bond market crash. The U.S. current account deficit was largely financed by Chinese dollars, which the country's authorities invested in U.S. Treasuries, agency bonds, and corporate bonds. If you hit the bondholders, the result could be a meltdown in the bond market, which would trigger the mother of all financial crises. It is not fair, for sure, to exempt the bondholders, given that the taxpayer has to finance the lion's share of the banks' irresponsibility. But the alternative might be worse.

The Obama Election

Back in the fall of 2008, the Americans employed TARP, and the Europeans chose to guarantee all bank credits, and to recapitalize banks on a voluntary basis. Both thought that would solve the crisis. It did not.

Barack Obama's election victory brought hope that a new administration, backed by a dual majority in Congress, would be able to bring relief to the situation. Obama announced the crisis would be his first priority, and after a couple of weeks of consultations, he appointed Timothy Geithner, hitherto president of the New York Federal Reserve, as Treasury Secretary; Larry Summers, a former Treasury secretary and academic, as director of the National Economic Council, whose job it is to coordinate economic policy across the administration; and Christina Romer, an economist from Berkeley, to the chair of the Council of Economic Advisers. These appointments were widely applauded, certainly among economists.

In early November 2008 it became clear that the financial crisis would have significant effects on the economy. The National Bureau for Economic Research declared that the U.S. recession had officially started in December 2007, based on a series of indicators, such as growth, production, and employment. Reports surfaced from manufacturing companies worldwide, warning about a sudden drop in orders. In the United States, the car industry found itself in trouble, and at one point it seemed likely that it might not make it until the holiday season. In Europe and Asia, too, this crisis suddenly began to affect the real economy, and at that point it became a political issue. But at the time, the vast majority of economists and forecasters still underestimated the extent of the crisis. Most of them still predicted a relatively mild recession, somewhere between "a garden variety" recession and an average recession, lasting a few quarters, with an accumulated loss of output of much less than 5 percent.

During November and December 2008, the global economy deteriorated at a pace not known since the Great Depression. In November, the volume of global trade collapsed. The CPB Netherlands Bureau for Economic Policy Analysis estimated that the fall in global trade volumes was 5.3 percent in November, and another 7 percent in December, and the same again in January 2009. In three months alone, global trade volumes were down 20 percent. That meant global trade volumes were falling faster than during the Great Depression. The estimates then for the fall in global trade volumes at the time were between 25 and 35 percent. These are volumes, not value. In value terms, global trade fell faster during the Great Depression, but this was mostly due to deflation, as the price of the goods themselves fell. While economists feared a return of deflation, there were no indications by February 2009 that prices would be falling on a sustained basis during the current downturn.

This massive fall in global trade was the proof that this crisis, which started in an obscure subsegment of the U.S. mortgage market, had developed into a full-fledged and synchronized global economic crisis, to a much greater extent than was previously envisaged. It was eerily synchronized. The classic trade surplus countries—China, Japan, and Germany—were hit particularly hard. In the fourth quarter, the Japanese economy had shrunk at an annualized rate of 13 percent, and Germany followed at 8 percent. The International Monetary Fund forecast in early 2009, that global trade would effectively stagnate, while the industrialized world would be in a recession. By February's end the economic news was still getting worse and worse; the global economy seemed to be in a free fall. There was discussion among economists whether the stimulus package would work or not. But there was agreement that their effect in 2009 would be limited. Fiscal policy did not come in early enough, and monetary policy lost traction. Despite the cuts in global interest rates, there was no increase in credit, as the banks cut credit volumes.

Trillions of Dollars

In the United States, the Federal Reserve effectively allowed short-term interest rates to fall to zero in November 2008, which was acknowledged officially the following month, when the Fed Funds Target rate was cut to 0 to 0.25 percent. The central bank hit what is known by economists as the "zero bound." Short-term interest rates cannot go below zero, and at that point the central bank has to deploy alternative measures to support the economy. So the Fed started what is known in the jargon as "printing money."

A central bank does not literally turn on the printing presses. What it does is buy bonds from banks, and simply credit the banks' reserves accounts, which are non-interest-bearing accounts that depository institutions have to hold with the Fed to satisfy its reserve requirements. So where does the Fed get the money to buy the bonds? This is the moment when it "prints the money." It simply credits the reserve accounts, and that is that.

Like a bank, the Federal Reserve also has a balance sheet. Following is an extremely simplified version, which suffices for our consideration.

Assets	Liabilities
Credits to financial institutions	Currency in circulation
Securities held	Bank reserves

As in our discussion with banks, it is best not to use a common-sense definition of assets and liabilities, but define assets as claims the central bank has on others, and liabilities as claims others have on the central bank. A $20 bill is a liability for a central bank, as the holder of the bill can demand that the Fed pays for his purchases. This sounds a little bit long-winded to explain a simple $20 purchase, but this is actually what a dollar bill does. A banknote is a promise by the central bank to pay up. In the United Kingdom, a £20 bill has a picture of the Queen and the words: "I promise to pay the bearer on demand the sum of twenty pounds." So it is not the banknote itself that is the money, but the promise it entails. It is, of course, a promise we have great faith in. This is also why we talk about dollar bills. Like a Treasury bill, a banknote is a paper issued by the authorities with a promise to pay. Unlike a Treasury bill, a banknote carries a zero interest rate (though Treasury bills' interest did fall to zero, and below, during this crisis).

So currency is clearly a liability for the central bank, and so are obviously bank reserves, the accounts commercial banks hold with the Fed. On the asset side, there are credits to the financial sector. When the Fed supplies the system with liquidity, this liquidity is credited under "bank reserves," as well as under "credit to financial institutions." It is a typical loan transaction. If I give you a loan, you have the money on your account, and at the same time you owe me the money. The balance sheet takes account of both.

We have already noted that the Federal Reserve and the European Central Bank have different ways in which they inject liquidity into the system. The Fed uses open market operations, through which it buys and sells various types of securities. A purchase of securities is recorded on the balance sheet under assets, as an increase in securities held, and under liabilities, as an increase in bank reserves, since the Fed credits the reserve account. The Europeans inject money into the system through a method known as securities repurchase agreements (repos) where the central bank purchases securities from a commercial bank for a fixed period of time.

This background suffices to understand what the Federal Reserve did when it switched to a policy known as quantitative easing, or credit easing. There are some subtle differences between the two. When interest rates hit the zero bound, it is an indicator that the central bank has used up its main policy instrument. It cannot provide additional stimulus by means of cutting interest rates further. But it can print money.

And this is how it works. The Fed deliberately boosts the size of its balance sheets by purchasing securities or extended credits to the banking sector. There are two ways to achieve this goal. The first is what Ben Bernanke christened "credit easing." Credit easing targets the asset side of the balance sheet. The principle idea is that if the central bank buys, for example, commercial papers—short-term debt instruments issued by companies—the banks will have an incentive to trade and issue such instruments. The purpose is to get those markets working again.

The alternative policy is "quantitative easing," which focuses on the liability side of the balance sheet. The Bank of Japan used quantitative easing during 2001 and 2006, and its focus was, looking again at our simplified balance sheet, to boost the reserve accounts to a certain level. Of course, liabilities are always equal to assets, so the two things accomplish the same in the end: There is more liquidity in the system. The difference is what side of the balance sheet you are specifically targeting. With credit easing, you are more interested in the composition of your assets. For example, if you want the banks to sell more mortgages, you might deliberately buy mortgage-backed securities from them. You may not have a quantitative target in terms of how you buy. You define your target in terms of how much the banks should lend. With quantitative easing, the goal is simply to print a certain amount of money, and inject it into the banking system, via the reserve accounts.

The Fed and other central banks have boosted their balance sheet from something around $700 billion to $2 trillion during the crisis, and the Fed's subsequently announced programs would probably boost it to an order of magnitude of $3 to $4 trillion.

The ECB has also increased its balance sheet, but less so, from something like €1200 billion to €1800 billion. In other words, the central banks printed a lot of money, by buying up all sorts of securities from banks. There will come a time when the central bank will have to take it all back, to "mop it up," as central bankers call it. This is easier said than done, because it involves taking a lot of liquidity out of the system at a time when the economy is recovering. The central banks will, without a doubt, be accused of killing an incipient economic boom. Yet failure to mop it up could lead to an increase in inflation. Both the Federal Reserve and the ECB are committed to maintaining a high degree of price stability. So there may be problems ahead as the economy moves out of recession.

A lot of economists and journalists can get very excited about interest rates, but in this crisis interest rates were not nearly as relevant as they normally are. The constraint faced by borrowers was not a price, i.e., an interest rate constraint, but a quantity constraint. The banks would not lend at *any* price, as they were busy cleaning up their own balance sheets. And the most effective way to take risk out of a balance sheet is simply not to lend. The main effort by central banks, and governments at the time, was to find ways of getting those banks to lend again. And this task proved very difficult indeed.

The TARP program did not succeed on political and economic grounds. It was unfair in that it bailed out the shareholders; but it was also not sufficient. It would not have solved the problem, which was much bigger than even many experts had thought. In early 2008, the IMF shocked the world with a forecast that the total estimated write-offs of toxic structural securities products would be some $1000 billion. In early January 2009, it raised the estimate to $2200 billion. Nouriel Roubini, a professor of economics at New York University's Stern School of Business, who had correctly forecast the extent of this crisis, produced an estimate of $3600 billion. About half of these write-offs are in the United States, in other words a total of $1100 billion and $1800 billion, depending on which forecast you are using. But the U.S. banking system only has a total capital of $1400 billion. If Professor Roubini's estimate is correct, this would suggest that the entire U.S. financial system would be insolvent. Remember our bank balance sheet. Any losses incurred reduce the size of the assets, and also the size of the capital. So these losses, or write-offs, come out of capital. In the more optimistic estimate, one would have to deduct losses of $1100 billion from capital of $1400 billion, which leaves only $300 billion. In this case, the U.S. banking system as a whole would be effectively insolvent, as this capital is insufficient on any realistic capital adequacy calculation, whether you are using Basle I or Basle II, or some other measure.

The situation was hardly better in the United Kingdom, or in Germany, where losses in banks also kept mounting. The fact was that large parts of the Western banking system were either insolvent, or de facto insolvent.

The trouble was that government had no effective responses. In the fall of 2008, programs such as TARP, or various European schemes to guarantee all bank lending and inject new capital into banks, had prevented an immediate catastrophe, but they had not solved the problem—which was to get the banks to lend again at more realistic levels. The world was looking at the incoming Obama administration for a solution. In his inaugural address on January 20, 2009, the new president said: "The state of our economy calls for action: bold and swift." The first priority of the administration was the stimulus package, the original version of which was both larger, and more weighted toward infrastructure spending. After a fight with Congress, a small but still substantial package was created, which came in at under $800 billion, composed of tax cuts and infrastructure spending. Germany, which had been reluctant to pass a stimulus package, eventually agreed on a package worth €50 billion, some $65 billion, but all these packages would not have much effect at all during the first half of 2009. Most of the effect of the stimulus would be expected for 2010.

Then the spotlight fell on the bank rescue package, which was supposed to be announced Monday, February 16, 2009. On the previous Sunday, the U.S. administration leaked the news that the package would not be announced until Tuesday. When it was announced on Tuesday, it became clear that Treasury Secretary Geithner did not actually present a worked-out plan, but more of a plan for a plan, or a list of principles. There would be no outright nationalization, but a public-private partnership. There would be stress-testing, an exercise in which federal regulators would walk into the bank, make some pessimistic assumptions about the future, and see how the bank would cope under such a scenario. This stress-test would determine how much more capital the bank would require. This would be provided by the government as well as the private sector. Geithner fiercely opposed nationalization. And so did President Obama, who said that nationalization was un-American.

To many observers, including this author, this plan failed to convince, because it was not clear how it would solve the problem; how the banking system could write off some $1100 billion to $1800 billion, and simultaneously have sufficient capital for normal operations to resume again. Nationalization, or the set of a bad bank, would have been a chance for an immediate fresh start. The government would wipe out the existing shareholders by injecting new capital. The nationalized banks would be resold at a later stage, while they would be restructured during the period of nationalization. It would be costly, but it would make it a possibility for the banks to lend again.

By early March, the situation had deteriorated significantly. The global economy's decline was much worse than originally feared. In Germany, the manufacturing sector was declining at an annualized rate of 50 percent. All over Asia, exports plunged some 40 to 50 percent over the previous year. While this was not yet the Great Depression, the speed with which global trade melted down was stronger than at any point during the 1929–1932 period—during which global trade volumes fell by an estimated 25 to 30 percent. If the rate of decline of the months November until January had continued, we would be there during the year 2009.

In early March the stock markets crashed, and then quickly recovered. The Dow Jones was headed in the direction of 6,000, and later moved upward almost 1,000 points. Figure 2.2 is a chart from the blog Calculated Risk.[2]

This big rally in mid-March—described by Nouriel Roubini as a suckers' rally—is no more than a little tick in the scheme of things. By that time, the S&P had fallen so much that it was on the same trajectory as the stock market was during 1929–1932.

Later that month, Geithner provided the details of his plan, and this time, the market liked it. The commentators were split. Roubini liked it, and so did the U.C. Berkeley economist Brad DeLong, who said that the $1 trillion public-private partnership scheme announced by Geithner would at the very least produce a lower price for the government than the original TARP scheme. If you add the Fed's asset purchases, the current stimulus, and a future stimulus, maybe this would be enough to unfreeze the credit markets. Other commentators were significantly more worried. Jeffrey Sachs commented that it was a

---

[2] http://www.calculatedriskblog.com.

Figure 2.2 Bar chart showing comparison of four bad bear markets in different crises.

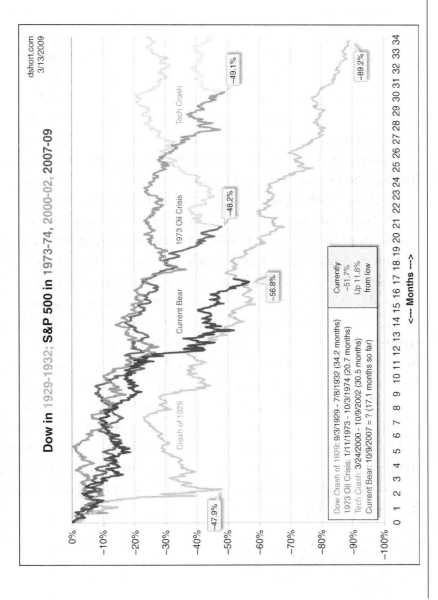

taxpayer rip-off, and Adam Posen, deputy director of the Peterson Institute for International Economics, said the situation reminded him of a similarly clever but futile attempt in Japan to clean up its banking system in the 1990s. In the end, the only thing that worked was the later decision by the Japanese government to force the banks to write down their debt. This author was also among the skeptics. The Geithner scheme appeared very clever, but clever in the sense that structured products are clever. It was not transparent. It was one-sided in that the private investors could hardly lose, and that alone would lead to subsequent problems, in particular political problems. If one needs to return to Congress to ask for additional money for a bank rescue, there is a risk that one might not get it.

Our narrative of the crisis ends at this point. The year 2009 was bound to be one of the worst years for the global economy in modern times. Back in the spring, some observers claimed to have spotted some green shoots of recovery. Those who are reading these words in the fall of 2009 or later will know better than the author and those earlier forecasters what really happened. We knew back in the spring that every recession, or depression, would end eventually. So would this one. The question is: How long will this recession last, and how bad will it be? And what comes after it? The author's best guess is that none of these questions—and certainly not the last—will have been answered by the fall of 2009. As economic downturns go, this one was truly scary.

CHAPTER 3

WHY DID IT HAPPEN, AND WHAT NOW?

The Causes

When asked about the impact on the French Revolution, the former Chinese premier Zhou Enlai famously answered: "It is too early to tell." The same can be said about the causes and consequences of this crisis. It took decades after the world gained a deeper understanding of the Great Depression. Of course, that does not mean that economists were clueless during the event itself. But during the crisis, most economists misunderstood it, and only a few had a partial understanding. Among the latter was the economist Irving Fisher, who developed an important insight in the fading days of the Great Depression, that debt and deflation fed on each other to produce a vicious cycle. It was known as the "debt-deflation theory." The British economist John Maynard Keynes was the first to produce a comprehensive explanation of the crisis that encompassed both the goods and the financial markets. One conclusion of the

Keynesian analysis was that monetary policy becomes ineffective in deep crises, and that fiscal policy becomes the instrument of choice. In the 1960s, Milton Friedman and Anna Schwartz postulated that the Great Depression was caused by monetary policy—central banks caused the crisis by shrinking the money supply. Other economists like Charles Kindleberger and Barry Eichengreen, attributed the Great Depression to the gold standard, which is probably the most widely accepted theory today. But there is still no such thing as a single theory of the cause of the Great Depression.

We should therefore not be surprised that we do not have a theory as to the cause of our own crisis yet. In fact, we do not even have what one might call an emerging consensus. We have many views instead, some more plausible, some less so. But when someone blames Alan Greenspan, or the banks, or whomever, chances are they have not thought about this complex issue in sufficient detail. U.S. monetary policy did play a role during this crisis, and, naturally, so did the banks, as we discussed in this book in some depth. But in examining this problem, we need to distinguish between deep causes, necessary factors, and coincidences. In this chapter, I am attempting to do this. Naturally, I make no claim of having found the universal truth of this crisis. The prediction I am most confident in making is that it will take years, if not decades, until we gain a deep understanding of this crisis. But I think I am in a position to disentangle the plausible from the implausible, and point to some of the issues.

The fact that this was a financial crisis does not logically mean that this was a crisis of finance, in the sense that it was caused by finance. Of course, it is true that banks and investors took on too much risk. It is also true that the rating agencies behaved in an irresponsible manner, and that the financial industry turned into a rent-extracting monster. But this only tells us what happened. It does not tell us why it happened. Let's go back to Martin Feldstein's six reasons for the crisis:

1. Excessively low interest rates
2. Bad financial regulation
3. Bad housing policies
4. Failure by rating agencies
5. Bad risk management
6. Excessive debt

I agree with this assessment, but it is little more than a description of crises. Whether these points are causes is a completely different matter. What caused the low interest rates? Do we really believe that the deep cause behind the low interest rates was a single central banker? What caused excessive risk-taking and debt? Obviously, one could go on and on with those questions, but people do not take on too much debt out of the blue. In the first part of this chapter, we will look at the six most popular suspects believed to be the causes of our current economic crisis:

1. Greedy bankers
2. Hedge funds and tax havens
3. Faulty risk models
4. Financial deregulation and lax supervision
5. Monetary policy
6. Global imbalances

Let us address each of these points in turn. They all contributed to the crisis. Of this, there is no doubt. But can they all be causes?

When Greed Is Not Good

Some people always get worked up when they hear that some banker earns dozens of millions of dollars a year. It is difficult to imagine that the endeavor of any human being, let alone a banker, could be so profound as to earn such compensation. I would agree with that proposition. My reaction has always been: let stupid shareholders pay however much they like to whomever. There is no way to justify such salaries. But then again, it is not my money. This was our ultimate consolation.

That, as it turned out, was a misjudgment. When the big banks and insurance companies got bailed out by their governments in New York, and in London, the top executives nevertheless insisted on their bonus payments. AIG, probably the most incompetent financial company of all time, had to be bailed out to the tune of $160 billion, and yet its executives felt they were entitled to several hundred million dollars worth of bonus payments. Of course, these bonuses were small relative to the sums involved in the rescue of the bank, but they symbolized the unfairness better than anything else. Bankers were so incompetent that they had to be bailed out by the government, and then they rewarded themselves for their failure. It is no surprise that this outrageous behavior has greatly contributed to what I call regulatory revenge. It may or may not be a good idea to levy surcharge taxes on bonus payments, but the financial industry has no right to complain. They handled the situation with such incompetence and insensitivity that this result is inevitable. They have left behind an incredible space of torched earth.

There is reason to suspect that the bonus system played an important role in this crisis. It created incentives for traders to take on excessive risks. If the risk resulted in failure, it was most likely to be a systemic failure. This means: Heads you win, tails you get bailed out. So this attitude was a clear example of privatizing gains and socializing losses.

But how could traders and their superiors take on such risks? The reason was they were in a unique position to extract high rents, as they were sitting on the sources of funds to finance the economy. Money and finance are catalysts for economic activity that would otherwise not take place. If, in an old-fashioned banking system, you run the only bank in town, you would be in a position to charge monopoly prices. Everybody would have to come to you.

The modern financial world was an oligopoly of a few large institutions. Most of the activity in the business for credit default swaps (CDSs)—a market with a notional value of some $62 billion at one time—was controlled by a group of ten banks. There was a handful of large investment banks, and a group of large global commercial banks that ran most of the business. Almost all the transactions in this transaction-oriented form of capitalism went through them. If you wanted an interest rate swap, chances were that the swap was organized by one of those large banks. Oligopolies can be fiercely competitive, but they generally do not produce ruinous price competition.

This was certainly the case in the financial sector, where chairmen habitually spent millions installing open fireplaces in their fiftieth-floor office suites, where executives and traders expected to receive large bonuses, to be paid early and on time each year.

Just think of how the bonus system worked in our credit bubble. Each year, the CDS market would more than double. Companies had no time to go bust, as one trader famously put it. The safest way to make money was to take on maximum risk. The more of these toxic papers you created, the bigger your profit, and the bigger your bonus. There was virtually no immediate risk in such transactions, and the long-term risk was not apparent. For as long as the bubble continued, the CDS Ponzi game worked.

The case for regulating bonus payments is therefore very clear. The system as it works at the moment produces the wrong incentives. It has what economists call negative externalities. The bonus payment may benefit the recipient, but it harms society by setting perverse incentives. The idea that bonus payments are needed to attract the best and the brightest is complete hogwash. These people were not bright, they were merely risk-loving. And taking on too much risk is never a smart idea.

The bonus system was an important factor in this crisis, and it certainly deserves our regulatory attention, to put it mildly. There is a strong case to tax these bonuses out of existence, or at the very least to create bonus systems that are far less extravagant, more long-term oriented, and most importantly, not procyclical.

But alas, the bonus system did not cause the financial crisis. It was in place long before this crisis erupted, long before the bubble. It was one of those many factors that contributed to the crisis. The current situation would have happened without it. As disgraceful as those bonuses may be, we should strike them off our list of fundamental causes.

Hedge Funds and Tax Havens

This is an issue more for Europeans than for Americans. I am going to deal with it briefly, as it highlights some aspects of the international debate. In some countries, notably in Germany, the political classes developed some strange narratives about this crisis. The German finance minister seemed convinced that unregulated hedge funds and tax havens were responsible for the crisis. I presume he was playing to a domestic audience, and tax evasion is a big issue over there. The idea was that the ultimate source of this racket is tax evasion, and this theft is recycled by hedge funds into the global economy.

In 2007, there were serious concerns about the stability of hedge funds. One conceivable crisis scenario at the time was the hypothetical bankruptcy of a hedge fund, which might bring down banks and other funds. It did not happen. And whatever one may think about the Cayman Islands, Liechtenstein, or the Channel Islands off the coast of the United Kingdom, the tax havens did not cause this crisis, and neither did the hedge funds.

The fact that we were even discussing these issues reflected the politics of the situation. The German government needed to blame someone, and the tax havens were a perfect target. It would be difficult to argue with the proposition that one should crack down on tax havens. Their business model is frankly pathetic, as it depends on depriving countries of legitimate tax revenues, and as they may even encourage the crime of tax evasion. But they had almost nothing to do with this crisis. To find the causes of this crisis, one must look elsewhere.

Financial Innovation and the Failure to See Risk

A fundamental problem of the credit market is that it is logically impossible to evaluate the inherent risks in a numerical way. The fact that people try time and again is part of the tragedy of this market. Avinash Persaud, a professor of finance, once made the observation that the risk models used in the financial industry critically depend on the fact that no one else uses them. The risk managers I have encountered tend to overestimate their ability to manage risk. In particular, they rely on faulty models which have proven to have failed in this crisis. And they continued to rely on these models even after the crash. Risk management is one of those modern oxymorons, a contradiction in terms, like self-regulation.

Behind risk management lies a large body of financial mathematics. In this section, I provide a nontechnical discussion of some of the complex issues involved while the accompanying sidebar gives some more technical details.

Mathematical innovation has clearly been one of the drivers of this crisis. Without our advance in financial mathematics we would never have had a market for credit derivatives. We might not even have had a large market for stock options. We would simply not have known how to price such securities in an efficient manner.

Ever since Fisher Black, Myron Scholes, and Robert Merton discovered the formula for determining the price of a stock option in the early 1970s—the Merton-Black-Scholes model—modern finance has increasingly become a discipline of applied mathematics. One of the building blocks of modern financial models is the mathematical theory of "stochastic processes"—sequences of events that are subject to chance. There are many types of stochastic processes, some of which are completely chaotic, and some of which are subject to some order.

Thus, for example, you could model the number of cars that arrive at a freeway junction with a stochastic process known as a Poisson process, named after the mathematician who discovered it. You do not know exactly when the next car comes, but there are things you know about this process. The number of cars arriving at a junction increases incrementally—one car arrives at a time. It never decreases (unless the cars are allowed to reverse back to your counter). You know that more cars arrive during rush hours than during the night, and so on.

And then there are smooth processes, which do not move upward incrementally as in the above example, but which move—up or down—perhaps by a fraction of a number. You can construct such processes in a way that they never become negative, or that they stop when they hit a certain point. Another type of stochastic process is one that could jump from one state to another. One would estimate that a stock market crash might be described by such a process.

The theory on which stochastic processes are based is among the most elegant theories in modern mathematics. These processes form the basis of modern financial models. When economists use a model to gain an insight into some reality, such a model is by definition a reduction of reality. The idea is that you can hopefully separate the important from the unimportant, to gain some insight, for example about where a stock price is heading, or where the economy is going. When you model some phenomenon, you always encounter a trade-off between simplicity on the one hand, and the desire to be as realistic on the other. When the model is too simplistic it might not explain what happened, but if it is too complicated, the model contains too much noise—just as reality contains too much noise. We all know that we have a financial crisis, but we do not immediately see why we have it.

When modeling a stock price, mathematicians use a stochastic process known as geometric Brownian motion, named after a Scottish botanist who tried to model the motion of gas molecules in the nineteenth century.

The Normal Distribution and Stock Prices

Brownian motion in the familiar two-dimensional plane can be represented in a typical coordinate chart: The x-axis of the process is time, and the y-axis is the process you want to model, say the price of a security. The progress begins at some point, let's say at $100. A moment later, it can be higher or lower, but the fluctuation from one point to the next is not entirely random. The extent to which the process can change from one time unit to the next is influenced by a probability law. The most frequently used probability law is the normal distribution. The normal distribution is the most important probability distribution in mathematics. The normal distribution is often drawn as a bell curve. Most events that happen are relatively close to the mean. Only a few events are far away from the mean. A surprisingly large number of natural events can be adequately described by the normal distribution, for example the intelligence quotient of a large and random group of people. Most people will have an IQ of around 100, some will have an IQ of between 80 and 120, but very few will have an IQ of between 50 and 150, and nobody will have an IQ of between 0 and 200.

In a stochastic process, you effectively throw a dice at each notch. But instead of a dice with six numbers, the outcome is determined by a probability law. In the case of an IQ, this probability law might give you 95, or it might yield 103, but it will not give you 0 or 200. The normal distribution is such a probability law. It has some dispersion, but nothing too extreme. If the normal distribution was really the correct probability law for stock prices, then the probability for a stock market crash to happen in 1987, 2001, and 2008–2009 is 1 divided by a number that is larger than the age of the universe. And as the economist Paul de Grauwe[1] has demonstrated, "larger" is an understatement.

(Continued)

---

[1] "How Abnormal was the Stock Market in October 2008?" Paul de Grauwe, Leonardo Iania, Pablo Rovira Kaltwasser, Eurointelligence, http://www .eurointelligence.com/article.581+M5f21b8d26a3.0.html

On the Web site Eurointelligence, de Grauwe wrote the following:

We selected the six largest daily percentage changes in the Dow Jones Industrial Average during October, and asked the question of how frequent these changes occur assuming that, as is commonly done in finance models, these events are normally distributed. The results were truly astonishing. There were two daily changes of more than 10 percent during the month. With a standard deviation of daily changes of 1.032 percent (computed over the period 1971–2008), movements of such a magnitude can occur only once every 73 to 603 trillion billion years. Since our universe, according to most physicists, exists a mere 20 billion years we, finance theorists, would have had to wait for another trillion universes before one such change could be observed. Yet it happened twice during the same month. A truly miraculous event. The other four changes during the same month of October have a somewhat higher frequency, but surely we did not expect these to happen in our lifetimes.

The normal distribution has a number of conveniences, which is the reason why it is so popular. It is easy to use. You can describe the normal distribution by only two values, the mean and the variance. Both mean and variance are special versions of what is known in mathematics as the *moments* of a distribution. The normal distribution is unique in that all its moments are finite. In a two-dimensional graph, the normal distribution is expressed in the form of a bell curve (see Figure 3.1).

Figure 3.1 Graph of a bell curve.

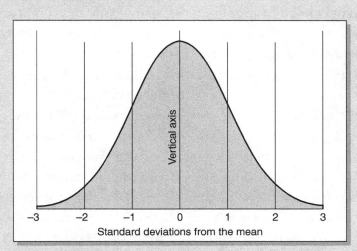

Standard deviations from the mean

In technical terms, in a normal distribution, 95 percent of values fall within two standard deviations of the mean. This means extreme cases exist, but they are very rare. A normal distribution is popular because it is easy to compute. It possesses a number of attractive mathematical characteristics, even if the mathematical formula for this distribution may be intimidating at first. Over long periods of time, it is possible for the process to oscillate around zero and then suddenly, when it hits a rare extreme value, to drift off into the positive or negative region. If you draw this process as a line, you will see it has no gaps, or sudden jumps. Nevertheless, if you look at this curve with a magnifying glass—a mathematical magnifying glass, that is—the curve is everything but smooth. For instance, the curve is not differentiable at any of its points. That means you cannot use the toolkit from

(Continued)

classic calculus, such as differentiation or integration. You need the toolkit from another part of mathematics. This part is called stochastic calculus, developed by the late Japanese mathematician K. Ito in the 1950s.

The Brownian process, in its original form, is not very well-suited to describe how securities change their price over time. Ordinary Brownian motion has no bounds. If you use it to model stock prices, the price could easily become negative, which we know cannot happen in reality. In other words, any realistic process that describes stocks requires a lower limit of zero. To accomplish this, geometric Brownian motion was created, which does in fact include this important characteristic. It is based on the exponential function. The exponential function e or exp to the power of something is always a positive number. If you put the Brownian motion into the superscript, you get a process that stays positive at all times.

But remember, the probability law that drives Brownian motion is the normal distribution. There are also researchers who take completely different approaches. One of them is the famous mathematician Benoît Mandelbrot, one of the founders of the mathematical discipline that is popular today, fractal geometry. Fractals are closely related to chaos theory. A fractal is a "self-similar" geometric object. When a segment is enlarged, the enlarged object appears similar to the original. This process can be continued at random. No matter how closely one approaches the object, it never becomes smooth.

There are examples in nature, such as coastlines, that appear ragged, no matter how closely one approaches the line. In mathematics, there is a famous set called the Cantor set, which is defined as a broken interval from zero to one, which perfectly replicates its structure at any magnification. If we infinitely magnify this set, we obtain an object that consists almost completely of holes. Thus, fractals are raw geometric objects, and the goal of fractal geometry is to eventually come to grips with these objects mathematically, such as by measuring them. Mandelbrot contributed greatly to the development of fractal geometry, and he played a key role in popularizing the discipline with his well-known book, *The Fractal Geometry of Nature*. Since the 1990s, Mandelbrot has been increasingly involved in the application of fractal geometry to the financial sector. In doing so, he is expanding the existing models to include "fractal" components. Thus, the price process on which a security is based is not determined by a normal geometric Brownian motion but by a fractal Brownian motion. In other words, an attempt is being made to integrate certain phenomena, with which we are familiar from the reality of the financial markets, into the models. We know, of course, that extreme situations occur more often than the models suggest. We also know that in financial markets, extreme situations often follow other extreme situations. In other words, this process has memory. With the help of fractal Brownian motion, it is possible to take these important aspects into account. There are some technical problems associated with these models so that they cannot be used right now. It remains to be seen whether this direction in research will ultimately yield usable models for the financial markets. However, it is already clear that the credit market crisis has reignited this discussion surrounding alternative mathematical models.

The Merton-Black-Scholes option pricing model, for which its creators earned the 1997 Nobel Prize in Economics, operates on the basis of geometric Brownian motion. In the 1990s, financial mathematicians extended this model to cover credit risk. This was a hugely important jump, without which our story would have taken a different turn. It is precisely these models that led to the false ratings in the credit market.

The reason why these models give us inaccurate results is not faulty mathematics. Rather, the problem lies in the underlying assumptions or axioms. To develop a usable model for the financial market, financial mathematicians must make a series of assumptions. For example, these models always, and wrongly, assume that financial markets are "complete." This is a technical term that means that for each state of the future, you can replicate that state through a combination of basic securities. Let's say you have a portfolio of securities, and you want to hedge your risk perfectly. For example you could buy a share, and hedge against a fall in the share by writing a call option on the share. Provided the prices of the call options are rational, you would make approximately the same return, no matter what happens to the share. You are perfectly hedged. Obviously you are not going to make money by pursuing such a strategy. But this is not the question here. The point is that you can construct a portfolio that covers all states of the world.

Financial markets are not necessarily complete. There is no way you could have produced a perfect hedge when the entire financial market collapses, when your counterparties do not pay up.

The models also assume rationality—an implicit assumption in almost all of economics. We all know that people are rational some of the time, but not always. This also means that these models do not function at all times. For example, it is almost impossible to create a bubble with a standard mathematical model. You would have to introduce some notion of irrationality, or even chaos. But pure chaos is not a good description of stock price either. Most of the time, stocks behave quite well—except when they don't.

Another assumption often used in these models is the normal distribution of stock prices. We discussed this assumption in the previous sidebar. The normal distribution may explain ordinary movements of financial prices most of the time, but it cannot explain extreme events. Security prices simply do not follow the normal distribution. But people use it because it is simple, and banks use it in their risk models. One of the most frequently used risk models is known as Value at Risk, or VaR. Most banks in the world treat VaR as their miracle weapon in risk management. VaR attempts, for example, to answer the following question: What is the biggest loss I can suffer within one day, at a 95 percent probability? In this case, VaR is stated as a sum of money that one believes could be lost in a worst-case scenario.

The problem with the normal distribution in risk management is particularly severe. The normal distribution tends to underestimate risky events by construction. And yet risk managers tend to rely on the VaR models in the illusion that they have some control and know their risk.

The French statistician René Carmona gave an example in his book on financial statistics that the choice of a different distribution can dramatically affect the outcome. In a concrete example, the VaR produced a result of 1.96

(the units are irrelevant for the purpose of this discussion). But if only a slightly different distribution is used—say, the Cauchy distribution—the VaR jumps to 12. Carmona says this example illustrates the sensitivity of the result to even the smallest change in the distribution. And it is no surprise that the choice is open to abuse.

When you confront practitioners with this example, they usually tell you: Yes we know, but we find it useful nevertheless. This tells me that these so-called practitioners do not know what they are talking about. This model does not add any additional information. You should not buy it.

It is no surprise therefore that risk managers lived under an illusion of false security. Most still do. As one of the founders of modern financial mathematics, Robert Merton, said, "The attempt to quantify risk has led to the existence of more overall risk in the system," because everyone feels safer than before and therefore takes greater risks. This important feedback loop is not taken into account in many risk models. It results in risk being permanently underestimated, and this is what fueled the credit boom even further. The sidebar following gives another example of how the reliance on a variant of the normal distribution—the Gaussian copula—can cause serious problems.

The Copula

In financial mathematics, the normal distribution is encountered on every corner. One important area is the modeling of the credit risks of groups of securities, such as those found in an index. This modeling employs a modern concept from statistics, the copula, a concept that was virtually unknown a decade ago but is becoming increasingly popular today.

In the previous section we described the normal distribution in some detail. What do we do when we want to determine several events at the same time, such as the risk that exactly three companies in an index of 30 stocks will go under within a specific time period?

To address this question, a little probability theory is needed. Let us assume that we are playing a simple game of dice—the first game with a single die, the second game with two dice. To transfer this game into a mathematical model, we use the concept of a random variable. When we throw a single die, the possible values of this variable range from one to six. In this case, the random variable is subject to a uniform distribution. This means the probability of each number being cast is equal.

Now let us throw two dice, and then add up the numbers. To this end, we need a two-dimensional random variable, which is subject to a multidimensional distribution, which is called the joint distribution. However, in a game called "sum of two dice," the random variable is no longer uniformly distributed. For example, the sum of two dice can never equal one. There is only one combination that produces the number two, which is two ones. There is also only one combination that produces the number 12, a six and a six. There are two combinations each that produce the numbers three and 11. The number seven can be portrayed in six

(Continued)

185

different ways. This example illustrates that the extreme values at both ends are rarely attained, while the median values of five, six, and seven appear more often. If you map the joint distribution, you can create something that approaches the Gaussian bell curve again.

Using the concepts of distribution and joint distribution, we can now define a copula. The copula is a joint distribution of uniformly distributed random variables. We have known about joint distributions for a long time. But a copula is a joint distribution with an important additional twist. It is constructed in such a way that the distribution of each component is normally distributed in an interval of zero to one. To work within the copula, in other words, you have to twist the joint distribution a little.

The Gaussian copula, and other copulas, are key elements in modern credit market mathematics. The model forms an integral part of software packages that are commonplace in the entire industry. Copulas are used throughout today's financial world, where they are treated as a miracle weapon.

However, the concept is controversial among mathematicians, just as the use of VaR is controversial among statisticians. The mathematician Thomas Mikosch has written a sharp critique on the misuse of the copula in financial mathematics, and has compared the instrument itself with the emperor's new clothes, a reference to Hans Christian Andersen's famous fairy tale. Mikosch writes, for example, that there is no intellectual justification for the assumption that the individual components must be uniformly distributed in the interval between zero and one. Mikosch is also critical of the fact that there are no robust statistical tests that demonstrate the stability of this method. According to Mikosch, the reason that the Gaussian copula is so popular is that it is relatively easy to use. It is easier to make calculations using normal distributions. The only problem, however, is that the outcome is completely misleading.

This example also demonstrates that financial mathematicians are making assumptions, once again, that do not necessarily apply in reality. That would not be a problem if the deviations were rare and small. But in our case they are frequent and catastrophic.

The problem is not in the mathematics itself. The models are inherently logical. The problem lies in the way mathematics is applied in concrete situations. Because many of the users do not understand the underlying mathematics, while many mathematicians have only a very simplified idea of how financial markets actually work, extremely dangerous misunderstandings occur. The mathematicians produce unrealistic models. The practitioners, in possession of these powerful tools, apply them without knowing what they are doing.

So after all this discussion about mathematics, does this leave financial innovation as a likely cause of the crisis? Financial innovation is clearly not a reason for the fall in interest rates, or the rise in real estate prices. But it might be an explanation of how the subprime crisis got so easily out of hand. Each of the participants, the banks, the credit rating agencies, the buyers of these products, and even professors of finance, who specialize in securitization, did not see it coming. And the reason they did not see it coming is clearly related to the way the industry persistently misjudged risk. And they misjudged risk because they all believed in models that universally failed to predict risk.

So yes, there is no question that a breakdown in risk management was more than just a factor of this crisis. It caused a credit bubble to get out of hand. Without it, the crisis would have been much less severe. But alas, it is not a plausible cause for the crisis itself.

Financial Regulation and Supervision

We lump these two factors together. Regulation is the set of rules an industry is subject to, and supervision is the implementation of those rules. Were the rules at fault? Of course, the Basle frameworks had many disadvantages. They encouraged procyclical behavior among banks, as banks were encouraged to create ever more loans when the economy performed well, and to reduce their loans when it did not.

We should remember the Basle framework was drawn up to ensure that banks had sufficient capital, and to ensure that minimum standards would prevail throughout the globe. The problem was with action to circumvent those rules—most importantly the ability to shift loans into off-balance sheet vehicles. Arguably this is worse than the hypothetical situation under which there would have been no rules whatsoever. Under the Basle rules every bank only had to make sure that it fulfilled the requirement of the formal capital requirements. No attempt was made by the banks to question whether they would survive a crash test, and their auditors never examined this either.

When banks used a credit default swap (CDS) to insure the default of a security, that security was no longer treated as risky, in other words, it was no longer included in the Basle capital adequacy calculation. But if the CDS itself was risky, then the bank would be in serious trouble. The original goal of CDSs was to disperse market risk, so that not a single bank would have to bear the risk, but the entire market. As it happened the reality was that the risk was concentrated among a very small number of players. Two of the largest players were Lehman Brothers and AIG. As it turned out AIG was the risk-absorber of last resort. Had the U.S. government not spent almost $200 billion to bail out this company, the world financial system would have collapsed. Everywhere in the world there were banks that insured their risky assets through CDSs written by AIG. CDSs were a product with the goal to seek risk dispersion. In the end, it produced risk concentration.

The failure to regulate CDSs was probably the biggest single mistake. As stated before, CDSs are economical insurance, and they should have been treated as insurance products. This means that the insurer would have to post sufficient collateral to meet the demand in full. That, of course, would have killed the CDS market. The securities industries and its powerful lobby managed to prevent regulation of these products, which were traded over the counter. The argument was that there was no need for regulation since all the participants in this transaction were large financial institutions. There were no investors to protect. But these arguments ignored the massive counterparty risk that was allowed to build up. There were indeed no innocent investors protect to, but rather taxpayers, who paid for the AIG rescue.

The rating agencies are, from an economic point of view, a strange creature. Their business model consists of taking money from the people they rate. The reality of this setup is not nearly as corrupt as it sounds. And in fact the business model has worked well for a long period of time. There were some reports about abuses, but the main problem with rating agencies was not alleged corruption, but the fact that the mathematical models did not function well.

Governments and central banks still rely heavily on these agencies, and it might perhaps be a good idea not to regulate them, but to deprive them of their semi-official role. Central banks, for example, base their decision on which collateral they accept on ratings. It is the combination of their semi-official status and the lack of regulation that causes the problem. The easiest solution would be to take them out of the equation. The alternative would be to regulate them. Either one of the two alternatives will eventually happen, and probably more. There is also a strong case for more transparency—for the rating agencies to publish the models which they use to apply a rating. Such transparency alone would probably go a long way to change their behavior.

Any lists of regulatory failure can be very long. The Europeans are keen to regulate hedge funds and tax havens, even though it is not clear to which extent both contributed to this crisis. There is now a recognition that regulation was too soft and that it was a mistake to allow large sections of the financial market to escape any form of regulation whatsoever. The regulatory pendulum tends to swing violently. There is now a great appetite on both sides of the Atlantic, for stricter regulation of financial companies, even of bonus payments. I have not the slightest doubt that we are moving from a period of chronic underregulation to a period of chronic overregulation, which will over time become subject to deregulation. Did deregulation cause the crisis? I think this is very unlikely. It might have provided a fertile ground for the crisis to develop, but we have no evidence that we can prevent financial bubbles through regulation. The Glass-Steagall Act was still mostly in place when the 1987 stock market bubble happened.

How about lax supervision? This is again one of those aspects where you could say that it certainly contributed, but probably not caused the crisis, as it would imply that strong supervision managed to quell such crises in the past. There is plenty of evidence of mortgage misselling, and plenty of evidence that the Fed as the supervisors looked the other way. Bernie Madoff's Ponzi scheme, which collapsed causing a damage of some $50 billion, was not entirely unknown to the Securities and Exchange Commission (SEC), but they chose to ignore the warnings. There are many examples of human failure in this area. But is it really plausible to attribute this crisis to lax supervision, or even to a combination of lax regulation and lax supervision? Surely, it is perfectly legitimate to crack down on some of those practices, such as bonus payments which are not merely indecently large, but which, more importantly, encourage excessive risk-taking. By all means, regulate those bonuses. But also understand that the bonuses did not cause this crisis, just as tax havens or hedge funds did not cause it.

There are many aspects of the supervisory system that need strengthening, no doubt, the single most important being what is called macro-prudential supervision, which allows policy-makers to assess whether the credit that is currently circulating in the economy could pose a systemic risk for the global financial system. Such macro-prudential supervision would involve the central banks in greater supervision, in countries where that is not the current case, including the United Kingdom. Such supervision should determine whether the failure of a single institution could lead to knock-on effects elsewhere. If macro-prudential supervision had been effectively applied in the past, it would probably have established that an excessive amount of risk in credit default swap contracts was concentrated in a single company, AIG. The purpose of macro-prudential supervision is to give supervisors a bigger picture. It is not enough to look only at a bank. The big risk to the financial system stems from how the financial players interact with each other. The absence of effective macro-risk management at the global level is clearly a failure that contributed to this crisis. But just as lack of police is not a cause of crime, lack of supervision is not a cause of this crisis.

It would clearly be useful to strengthen the regulatory system, and to hire better-trained supervisors, and to increase their number. But we should not confuse what we all think might be a useful lesson but what we think caused the crisis. The bonus was in place in the 1990s, and earlier, and it did not cause a crisis then. The rating agencies have been around since the early twentieth century, and for most of the time, there was not a problem. The supervisory system has hardly changed over the years. These are all contributing factors to the current economic crisis, but they are not the cause.

The Role of Monetary Policy

One of the most frequently heard theories about this crisis is that it was caused by Alan Greenspan's decision to cut interest rates in 2003 to 1 percent, a level at which they remained until 2004. A more sophisticated version of this argument does not focus a single decision by a single central bank, but on the monetary policy stance of the Federal Reserve (the Fed) and other central banks since the mid-1990s.

It is true that low interest rates preceded the property and credit bubbles. Monetary policy is thus a plausible candidate for a cause. But simple time coincidence does not prove anything. It is possible that low interest rates and the property bubble were both caused by something else, or that the property bubble would have occurred without low interest rates.

To establish a causal link, we have to be sure that in the absence of a lax monetary policy, the bubble would not have happened at all. And I am very confident to predict that if the Fed stopped the interest rate cycle at 2 percent, rather than 1 percent, while more appropriate, it would not have made a fundamental difference. It might have shaved off a few percentage points in house price rises.

Conversely, of course, monetary policy can prick any bubble. It is a brutish mechanism. In fact, monetary policy did prick the U.S. property bubble. When interest rates went up again to peak at 5.25 percent, the U.S. property boom was truly over. The boom depended on interest rates remaining extremely low forever. But this is not the same as saying that the decision to cut interest rates to 1 percent caused the boom. And the housing boom started well before that decision—though it took off further when interest rates came down, and some time after that as well.

A similar debate about monetary policy as a cause of a crisis raged about the Great Depression. Milton Friedman and Anna Schwartz' *Monetary History of the United States* leaves no doubt that monetary policy was the singular cause of the Great Depression. This is very different from the mainstream view about the Great Depression, in which monetary policy clearly aggravated and prolonged the Great Depression, but did not cause it. Friedman and Schwartz argued that the Great Depression was the consequence of a shrinking money supply. So as long as central banks ensure that money supply can grow at a steady rate, neither bubbles nor depressions can happen.

We have long passed the heated monetarism debates of the 1960s and 1970s. The consensus among economists today is that money indeed causes inflation (or deflation) "with long and variable lags." This means that changes in the money supply are indeed the deep causes for shocks to price stability, but the relationship has become so confusing and complicated, especially in the presence of sophisticated money-gobbling financial markets, that the money supply is of little predictive value. Not only do we not know how long the lag is, its unknown length is going to change over time. Talk about unknown unknowns!

Modern macroeconomic models no longer treat money supply as an explicit variable. In fact, they do not even incorporate a financial market at all. In these models, the only monetary variable that counts at all is the short-term interest rates—the policy rate controlled by the central banks themselves. One type of such model—the so-called "dynamic stochastic general equilibrium model"—is used by many central banks for economic forecasting all over the world. Most of these central banks pursue policies of direct inflation targeting, in which they try to keep a measure of consumer price inflation within a certain range. Another use of these modern economic models is to forecast the future rate of inflation.

The Federal Reserve and the European Central Bank are also *de facto* inflation targeters, though both have other parameters they must take into account. The Fed has to pursue the goal of maintaining price stability as well as to secure a high level of employment, while the European Central Bank—which defined price stability in terms of an inflation target—uses monetary indicators to a stronger degree than other central banks.

But in all cases, central banks more or less target inflation—this means they target the changes in prices of a basket of goods. There are narrow baskets, such as the one that underlies the core inflation measure in the United States, which excludes food and oil. There are technical reasons why a central bank would choose to do so. The Europeans target a slightly broader basket. But no basket in the world could take sufficient account of the kind of house price increases we have observed in the United States and several other countries. Consumer prices were perfectly well behaved. In 2007 and 2008 there was some inflation in the system, but most resulted from higher oil and commodity prices. This was only very indirectly related to the bubble. In our bubble years, consumer prices were largely stable—helped by very inexpensive Asian imports—while asset prices shot through the roof. And the central banks only care about consumer prices. And this is why they kept interest rates low.

Could this single-minded focus on consumer prices, and the central banks' conscious decision to ignore asset prices, be a factor in this crisis? You could picture the economy like a giant waterworks. If you pour too much water into the system, you will experience some overflow in some other part of the system—if it is not consumer prices, then it is asset prices. Hydraulics makes for some very nice and frequently used metaphors in monetary economics, but is probably not an accurate way to imagine how a complex economy with a complex financial market works. This is precisely the same reason why we can no longer rely on a single variable—the supply of money.

As difficult as it is to formulate a coherent theory about why prices in an economy rise, it is even more difficult for economists to determine how, when, and why bubbles arise. There exists no complete, let alone widely accepted, economic theory of bubbles. In some cases expansion of the money supply may have contributed to a bubble, and in other cases a bubble was caused by something other than the expansion of money. Japan, for example, experienced a gigantic property bubble in the 1980s, and the money supply in the preceding period was not excessively expansionary.

Even if you believe that money, and money alone, can explain why prices rise or fall, it is still not clear why that should apply to asset prices as well. Asset prices and goods prices are not strictly comparable. In financial terms, an asset is a store of value and a promise to some future payment stream. A rise in asset prices therefore reflects a change in future expectations. Assets bubbles have quite a lot to do with mass psychology, and many aspects of a bubble lie beyond the realm of what classic economics can explain. And it is quite possible that several factors have to come together for a bubble of this kind to emerge—monetary policy being one of them.

But the evidence is not strong that monetary policy on its own could have been a plausible single cause for the bubble. But monetary policy could still be the lead player in a multiple-cause setup, where several factors together are responsible. For example, we might get a little closer to the truth if we take into account how monetary policy and the financial system interact.

For example, if a central bank in Japan keeps short-term interest at zero, while short-term interest rates in Europe are 4 percent, you create relatively risk-free, carry-trade gambles for players with access to large amounts to central bank money, such as banks, or hedge funds with open credit lines to banks. These investors borrow money at the zero interest rate in Japan, invest it in the European overnight money market, and make money for as long as the exchange rate does not move. Those investments would be hugely leveraged. The higher you leverage, the greater your profit. In fact, your access to borrowed money is the main determinant of your profits.

The downside of your gamble is a systemic risk. Should you lose through a massive overnight yen appreciation, chances are you are not the only loser. If you lose, so will many others, and the result would be a financial crisis, which the authorities would probably avert through currency intervention. With short-term interest rates at zero, a lot of really dumb bets suddenly seem very attractive. When interest rates are low, and when a central bank credibly promises to keep them low for a long time, then financial market activity is likely to increase sharply. More money will chase around the system. And this means lots of liquidity in the system.

In this scenario, the critical ingredient is huge gaps in interest rates between very liquid markets, such as Japan's and Europe's in our example, plus infinite access by hedge funds to central bank money. But these conditions are generally not met. For this scenario to work you need both an irresponsible monetary policy interacting with an irresponsible financial system. I am not sure how this dynamism captures the situation in full, but it possibly offers a partial explanation.

Global Imbalances

Apart from low interest rates, the persistent influx of capital from Asia into the United States played a decisive role as well. This may not only be a crisis for monetary policy, but a crisis of modern macroeconomics on a wider scale.

Experts have long argued over global imbalances. It was a subject that provoked intense discussion in academic and policy conferences for many years before the crisis. The debate subsided a little, as news about the credit markets took center stage. A leading U.S. policymaker told this author that global imbalance has played virtually no role in the day-to-day reality of international economic policy management, and in his judgment there is no chance that it will do so in the foreseeable future. I think he is wrong. Just because the problem was not being addressed does not mean it was resolved. Quite to the contrary.

What are global imbalances? An imbalance occurs, for example, when trade deficits or surpluses reach a very high level in certain countries without being offset by countervailing movements of exchange rates. In the years before the crisis, the U.S. current account deficit grew to over 6 percent of gross domestic product. The balance of payments consists of three parts: the balance of trade on physical goods, the balance of services, and the balance of transfers. The first two are the most important components in most industrialized countries. Transfers include, for example, money that individuals who live in foreign countries send to their home countries.

In some emerging economies, current account deficits are much higher than in the United States. In Turkey, for example, they accounted for 9 percent in 2007. Now there is no rule that says that a current account deficit cannot exceed a specific level. Various factors determine the sustainability of a current account position. In Turkey and other emerging nations, the current account deficit is often attributable to a high level of direct investment by foreigners. In this sense, the current deficit is more a sign of a country's attractiveness. In the United States, the deficit is mainly the result of domestic consumption of foreign imports, primarily from Asia. This too is not necessarily a bad thing, provided it is sustainable. There are even people who say that the Americans are the consumers of last resort. Without the voracious American consumers, the Asians would never have gone through an economic miracle of such scale.

For this reason, we will not treat current account deficits as a poor moral choice, as some people do, but purely as an economic fact of life. In the United States, an imbalance of 6 percent of GDP, which was the case until recently, is not sustainable from an economic point of view. At some point, the imbalances are offset by other factors, such as the weakening of the currency. The sharp decline of the dollar in 2007 and 2008 was taken as a sign that the imbalances were being reduced, but a subsequent revaluation partially reversed this process.

There is a yet another way of looking at the current account deficit. When China ships goods to the United States, the Americans must pay for them with dollars. These dollars flow from the United States to China. If you look at money flows only from a national accounting perspective, they are the reverse of the goods flows. Goods flow from China to the United States, the money flows from the United States to China. A U.S. current account deficit means a capital accounts surplus, and in China it is the very opposite.

Those flows to China exceeded the country's capacity to invest them domestically, and so China developed enormous foreign currency reserves. In 2007, China held foreign currency reserves of $1,300 billion. A year later, they rose to $2,000 billion. What is China doing with all this money?

The Chinese have invested much of the money back in the United States, mostly in U.S. Treasury securities, and increasingly in riskier forms of investment, as well. Like other surplus countries, China has established government-owned funds for the purpose of investing in foreign securities. The Chinese made their most spectacular investment in 2007 when they bought an 8 percent share in Blackstone, an American private equity firm, for $3 billion. The oil-producing countries are also accumulating large amounts of foreign currency reserves, which they invest primarily in the dollar zone, because the price of oil is quoted and paid in dollars.

Moderate current account deficits are generally not a problem. In classic international macroeconomics, the exchange rate is the main adjustment mechanism. If the United States runs a current account deficit, the dollar would subsequently rise in value, which would restore balance as U.S. exports become cheaper, and imports become more expensive. In theory, this process continues until balance is restored. The problem, however, is that this is not the way currencies behave in real life. China and many other countries have pegged their currencies to the dollar, either officially or unofficially. Most of these countries are those with which the U.S. trade deficit is particularly high.

The dollar strength is also upheld by large inflows of central banks. By reinvesting much of their surplus dollars in the United States, the Chinese support both the dollar and the price of U.S. Treasury securities. The effect of these foreign transactions on the yields of U.S. Treasury securities is estimated at up to half a percentage point. In other words, if dollar-rich emerging economies were not buying U.S. Treasuries in such large amounts, a 3 percent interest rate on a ten-year Treasury bond would in fact be 3.5 percent.

If the exchange rate does not work as an adjustment mechanism, what are the alternatives? Economists Maurice Obstfeld and Kenneth Rogoff, two of the best-known experts in the field of international economics, came up with the following scenario in 2005, when they argued that the U.S. housing bubble would burst, which would bring down domestic consumption, and ultimately cause a decline in the dollar's exchange rate. They got the mechanism exactly right. A housing bubble indeed led to an avalanche of events that brought about the adjustment.

This scenario leads to recession, and possibly worse. Rising unemployment prompts Americans to start saving more and consuming less. The demand for imported goods suddenly declines, as does the demand for American securities. These shifts, in return, lead to a decline in the dollar. Over time, this makes American products more competitive in global markets once again, and the old mechanisms are back in force. The current account deficit then normalizes again.

The debate over the causes of global imbalances is very important to us for two reasons. If the global financial crisis collides with global imbalances, the world economy is forced to undergo two simultaneous very large adjustment processes, which in turn could aggravate the crisis. But there is also another reason: the direct relationship between the imbalances and liquidity. There are many theories on the causes of liquidity bubbles, which are essentially nothing else but a discussion of the causes of the global imbalances. The imbalances, caused by the American current account deficit and the current account surpluses of the booming economies of Asia and the Middle East, produce large capital flows. It is precisely these flows of capital that give us the illusion of abundant liquidity.

When the bubble burst, the entire process moved into reverse. The markets dried up, the dollar lost value, and suddenly the liquidity was gone. For this reason, the topics of liquidity bubbles and global imbalances are closely related. This is a subject of vigorous discussion among international economists, but one that has yet to produce a consensus.

The most famous theory about global imbalances is the Bretton Woods II theory. It stems from economists Michael Dooley, David Folkerts-Landau, and Peter Garber, who theorized that global imbalances are the result of many of the newly industrialized countries having pegged their exchange rates to the dollar, just as Europe and Japan did until the collapse of the old Bretton Woods system in the early 1970s.

The authors argued that what many condemned as global imbalances was essentially a good thing. They believed that without Bretton Woods II, China and India would never have achieved their phenomenal growth rates. Many eminent economists agree with variations on this theory, including Robert Mundell, who won the Nobel Prize for his groundbreaking work on so-called "optimum currency areas." Bretton Woods II is now seen as one of the causes of the current crisis.

Overall, two major categories of approach to explaining the crisis have emerged: real economy arguments and monetary arguments. This is in some way reminiscent of the conflict between Keynesians and monetarists in the 1960s and 1970s, although today this is less of an ideological conflict but a debate over the way our globalized economy works.

The proponents of the real economy theories see the causes either in undesirable economic developments in the United States (deficits) or in spectacular growth in Asia. Although the emerging Asian economies are growing, they do not invest their profits at home, but in the United States.

This behavior on the part of the Asians means that the mechanisms that would normally reduce imbalances are not working. To put it simply, the Chinese and the Americans have entered into a Faustian pact. The Chinese run current account surpluses helped by an undervalued currency in a semi-fixed exchange rate system, through which they enable the Americans to live far beyond their means by keeping U.S. interest rates articificially low in return. The logic is not unlike the logic of a synthetic CDO. It is too good to be true. From the American standpoint, this simply means: We are helping the rest of the world by consuming as much money as possible.

The Bretton Woods II theory is ultimately an attempt to provide an intellectual justification of this perpetual motion. In the original Bretton Woods system, Germany played the role China plays today. The currencies of all member states in the system were fixed relative to one another. However, wage increases and inflation were lower in Germany than in other countries, allowing the country to continually improve its competitive position. Or as economists say: Germany experienced a real devaluation. Of course, it was not a nominal devaluation, because, in the Bretton Woods system, the external value of the Deutsche Mark was pegged to the dollar.

Bretton Woods lasted for a long time, but it eventually collapsed precisely because global imbalances had become too large. In the end, the German Mark appreciated while the value of the dollar declined. We are experiencing precisely the same process once again today. The number of countries with currencies pegged to the dollar has gone down in the last ten years. The value of the dollar has been declining since the early part of the crisis—though it has subsequently appreciated. Although China's currency, the Renminbi, is not officially pegged to the dollar, its exchange rate remains within close proximity to that of the dollar.

The relationship between Japan and the rest of the world represents another imbalance. After more than a decade of economic stagnation and falling prices, Japan's central bank, the Bank of Japan, embarked on a monetary policy based on interest rates being close to zero, whereas rates were higher in the rest of the world. This gap was persistent in the years before the crisis, and has since closed. That gap led to massive flows of capital backwards and forwards in the global financial system.

The gamblers were not only western hedge funds. Japanese housewives were also among them. They invested their leftover household money in Japanese funds, which then played precisely the same game. The funds took the money, augmented it with even more capital borrowed domestically at low rates, and invested the total in countries with higher interest rates.

Another example is the surplus of oil-rich countries that are reinvested in the West. In all these cases, imbalances produced speculative financial flows that were channelled through the large global financial centers—New York, London, and Zurich.

Robert Mundell says global imbalances are a sort of fuel for the world economy. According to Mundell, it would be fatal for us to attempt to dismantle the imbalances at this point.

Whether we like it not, the dismantlement of imbalances has begun. The dollar's loss of value is part of this process (since reversed, and reversed again). Moreover, there was already a significant decline in U.S. imports in 2008, while exports began to rise.

Now look how these flows interacted with American and European monetary policy. By investing huge surpluses into U.S. Treasuries, the Chinese effectively lowered the yield on U.S. bonds. The effect may have been as large as 0.5 percent.

This constant demand for U.S. fixed-interest securities allowed the Fed to keep interest rates lower than would otherwise have been the case. Alan Greenspan cut interest rates to 1 percent, not because there was an overwhelming need, but because he could. Some hyperventilating economists warned back in 2003 that the United States was about to fall into deflation, just because the inflation rate temporarily declined, and despite the fact that the economic growth rate was actually quite strong. That provided the intellectual backdrop to a decision that was based purely on opportunism. Interest rates were so low because the Chinese made it possible. And it is no surprise that when real interest rates were effectively zero or negative, a massive consumer-driven property bubble got completely out of hand.

This bubble was caused by global imbalances, reinforced by excessively loose monetary policies, and the way both interacted with a deficient financial market. Imbalances are the deep roots of this crisis—the original sin. But imbalances would never have developed their full toxic force without dysfunctional financial markets.

Solutions

The banking crisis presents a serious challenge for economic policy, to put it mildly. It appeared for a long time that policymakers were completely overwhelmed with the two big tasks ahead—stabilizing the current crisis and fixing the regulatory system. During the winter and spring of 2009 there was a big debate about what short-term measures were

appropriate. Some economists advocated large stimulus packages coordinated on a global scale. Others were skeptical. Some
economists favored a policy to nationalize and restructure the
banks, by closing down the bad ones and recapitalizing the
good ones. Treasury Secretary Geithner produced a bank rescue plan, of which it was not clear whether it would succeed
or not.

It makes little sense for me to discuss these important issues
in this book beyond what was already said in the earlier chapters. The reader in the fall or winter of 2009–2010 will know
whether the Geithner plan has succeeded or not, and whether
the stimulus packages worked or not.

What I can say with some confidence is that, from the perspective of spring 2009, we will not end this crisis unless we
restore health to the financial sector. This requires a determined policy response. An important lesson from Japan's lost
decade in the 1990s is the need to tackle the structural problems
in the financial sector. We have to get the banks to write off the
toxic assets, and to recapitalize and shrink the banking sector in
the process. If we have not done this by the time you read this
book, we will still have to do this in the future. And the longer
we wait, the longer will the recovery be delayed, and the more
serious the economic downturn threatens to be. Even the banks
benefit greatly from the Fed's program of quantitative easing,
however, this will not solve the problem on its own. We need
to force the banks to get rid of their dodgy debt securities.

In the following narrative, I will focus on the long-term
issues arising out of this crisis. Before we demand the sum-
mary execution of all bankers, it is a good idea to draw up our
list of recommendations with a view to the previous analysis of

causes and contributing factors. An action plan should address the causes first and foremost, but should also encompass the other factors.

In this book, we have examined two classes of causes. One class consists of macroeconomic causes, essentially global imbalances and monetary policy. The other deals largely with regulation and prudential supervision.

A well-designed regulatory framework should ensure that financial institutions are robust when confronted with economic shocks, financial innovation, regulatory arbitrage, as well as higher than average asset price volatility. The standard response is for long lists of regulatory measures, based on the analysis of what went wrong. In doing so, we almost always focus on the present crisis, believing that the next crisis will be similar. This is why I believe it is better to focus on principles and incentives, and to eschew the attempt to regulate everything in great detail. The next crisis may be in payment systems, or in foreign exchange, or in some place where we least suspect it.

It is therefore important that we prioritize reform on areas affecting the efficient function of the financial system as a whole. As this crisis was caused by an interaction of economic and financial factors, the following list encompasses recommendations that address both. I begin with the financial system.

Proposals for Financial Reform

1. The single most appropriate measure is to institute an effective and globally coordinated system of macro-prudential supervision, linking central banks and

supervisors, and allowing policymakers to instruct regulators to pull the plug—and to do all this across-border. A global credit register would be a useful start to improve transparency. It would require data exchange, at a very deep level, between the world's largest financial centers—New York, Chicago, London, Paris, Frankfurt, Zurich, Milan, and Tokyo.

2. We must ensure that no financial institution is too large to fail. And this means that we must impose explicit ceilings on the overall size of financial institutions. (This is more important than setting maximum leverage ratios, which is very problematic.) As for existing too-large-to-fail institutions we should subject them to a special regulatory regime with a view to breaking them up into smaller units. Concretely, we could require a financial institution not to accumulate assets beyond a certain threshold of the host country's annual GDP.

3. Since finance is global, we must pay serious attention to global forms of governance. This is not something we can achieve overnight. It will take years, if not decades, to establish such a system. But without such a system, financial globalization, and globalization in general, will otherwise retreat. In recognition of the global flows of finance, we should adopt a three-stage proposal to establish, successively:

  a. Global cooperation, and more effective exchange of information.

  b. Joint rule-making with national implementation.

  c. A degree of global implementation by a global regulator, yet to be established.

4. Global coordination and cooperation are necessary for any effective regulatory and supervisory system to work in practice. Otherwise, financial institutions will engage in cross-border regulatory arbitrage, and we would be back to where we started from. To the extent that global regulation is not immediately realistic, we should adopt intraregional regulation, for example, at the European Union (EU) or Asian level—and then coordinate policy within the blocks. For the EU in particular, this involves moving to a system where the largest banks are supervised by a central authority. The EU is currently considering proposals for supervisory reform, which may be a first step in this direction, but which is not going far enough to neutralize the grip of national governments on the regulatory system.

5. It is worth noting that this view is not universally shared by all. Dani Rodrik, professor of political economy at Harvard, believes global governance is unrealistic, as the world lacks both the infrastructure and the will to create it. The best option in his view is to optimize national regulations, and cooperate internationally. I personally think his view is too pessimistic, and if he is right, I think it would have disturbing implications. A world with large flows of goods, capital, and labor will need more than coordination between national governments; it will need a joint set of rules and some form of global-level democracy.

6. Another problem was the introduction of "mark-to-market" accounting rules in the early 1990s, which allowed companies to account for their assets based on market value. This rule is hugely procyclical. It means

that, in good years, banks can post additional gains because their assets have risen in value. By the same token, they post losses in bad years, so that these rules act in a pro-cyclical way. This was a serious problem, especially during the October 2008 stock market crash. If the accounting rules had not been temporarily relaxed, many banks and insurance companies would have had to file for bankruptcy.

7. Finally, moving to the macro-prudential regulations, the most important regulatory principle that should be adopted is what I call "the principle of economic intent." It means that we should not draw up long legal rules that try to anticipate every circumstance, something that can always be circumvented given a sufficient degree of ill will. Instead one should introduce an element of constructive ambiguity into the system by allowing supervisors to use economic analysis in their decision-making.

An example: A credit default swap (CDS) may be technically a swap, but it is economically insurance. It should thus be regulated like an insurance market, unless it is traded on regulated exchanges, in which case the exchange regulator is responsible. The rule would obviate any need to pass complex regulation about how to push the CDS market on to a regulated exchange. It would happen naturally, if an insurance regulator was entitled to regulate everything he or she regards as insurance.

Another example: If banks seek "regulatory relief" through the use of securitization, this should be regarded for what it is—a purely legal trick that does not change the underlying economics. Regulators should thus be empowered to force banks to bring off-balance sheet vehicles back onto the balance sheet.

8. Concerning the regulation of rating agencies. I would follow the advice of Charles Goodhart's roundtable of financial economists.

a. Make the rating agencies' mathematical models transparent.

b. Governments, central banks, and other public sector institutions should refrain from using rating agencies in an official capacity. Central banks should not value collateral on the basis of ratings, for example. If we want "official" ratings, we ought to create government institutions that provide them. If not, we must deprive the rating agencies of any official character. This would be an elegant solution to the problem of rating agencies, because it would downgrade them to the role of financial journalists. They could continue to pursue the freedom of opinion they hold in such high esteem, but would probably be doing so with somewhat lower profit margins.

c. In the rating of securitized products, rating agencies should publish a margin of error depending on leverage of the securitized structure.

9. Regarding specific market reform, one of the priorities should be, and already is, the establishment of new rules governing the market for credit default swaps (CDSs).

a. First, we must ensure that financial companies that write these instruments have sufficient collateral to survive a severe stress situation.

b. Second, we should seriously consider not allowing naked short-selling, i.e., insurance on bonds that the buyer of the insurance does not own. CDSs can be very dangerous instruments when abused, and naked short-selling is pure speculatation.

c. And finally, it would be advantageous to move the CDS market onto a regulated exchange. This is more than simply offering central-counterparty services. In doing so, you kill much of the present market, and that is probably a good thing too.

10. The Basle rules need to be replaced. This is a complicated subject, and the introduction of Basle III may not be the right answer. Some commentators have suggested that simple rules are superior to complicated ones, and this would mean that Basle I may have been superior to Basle II. We must find a way to ensure that banks are adequately capitalized, and to construct a system that is stable and not too procyclical. Avinash Persaud and others have also suggested that one should add liquidity as another dimension to those rules. Basle is only about solvency risk. There are no international rules to set minimum standards for liquidity. These discussions will keep a lot of economists and central bankers busy for many years to come.

11. Reform the bonus system. This is inevitable if only for political reasons after the AIG debacle, when the insurance company's executives added insult to injury by awarding themselves mega-bonuses despite their catastrophic performance. But politics alone does not justify regulation. The problem with the bonus system is negative

externalities. It was an important element of process that encouraged excessive risk-taking.

This list could be made even longer—and no doubt it will be made even longer. We could also start looking for pseudo-problems. A banker once told me that the problem is not the banks but the press, because of its habit of making everything public. I thought it was a fairly audacious remark, coming from a banker. We are always quick to castigate a free press. But the bankers weren't exactly complaining when a noncritical press hyped the bubble, as it always does. The capacity for denial and the lack of self-criticism among bankers is one of the characteristic features of this crisis. Perhaps one should shoot them after all.

Then again, perhaps not. As I have argued, even if there is misconduct and stupidity, this is not the root cause of a crisis. In other words, this crisis would have happened without the stupid bankers.

The Consequences for Macroeconomic Policy

If you believe, as I do, that the crisis is fundamentally caused by macroeconomic factors, we obviously need to prioritize those.

If economic imbalances are the cause of this crisis, we have to ensure that such imbalances do not return. This is not the same as saying we have to rebalance the economy. The latter is probably not necessary because it is already happening. As President Richard Nixon's economic advisor Herb Stein famously said: Something that cannot go on, won't. By this he meant that one does not need to stop an unsustainable development. It ends by itself. The same goes for global imbalances. To restore balance after the crash requires little, if any, policy action. In fact, maintaining those imbalances would require a massive political effort on all sides. Since the household sector in the United States is no longer in a position to take on new debt, or to consume imported goods in the same quantities as before, it would take massive government intervention—much beyond recent stimulus packages—to replace the shortfall in private sector demand.

A more balanced world might be a different one from the one we know. A world with less money flowing around, a world with less leverage, is also a world with fewer loans and less growth. We have to understand that global growth rates of 5 percent, which we were getting used to, may not be attainable under conditions of stability and global balance.

Even though rebalance will happen automatically, we have to ensure that the process that led to global imbalances does not return. As we identified our system of free-floating exchange rates between some currencies (notably dollar, euro, yen, and pound sterling), and Bretton Woods II–style arrangements between others (dollar, several Asian currencies, including China's, Middle Eastern, and Latin American currencies) as a cause for this crisis, it is time to fix this system. A return to the old Bretton Woods system of semi-fixed rates is not the answer, as that also led to unsustainable policies. The priority is not so much monetary regime change, but monetary regime management. Here is my list of macroeconomic policy priorities:

1. *Cooperation among central banks and Treasuries to prevent currency overshooting.* This could take the form of pre-announced target bands, or some less transparent arrangements, but with the clear goal of preventing and counteracting excessive exchange rate fluctuations.

2. *Cooperation among global central banks in monetary management.* There is increasing evidence that central banks are losing the grip on domestic policy, as both financial and price stability, two of a central bank's most important targets, are increasingly determined by factors outside the national borders and outside the central bank's control. Disinflation during the 1990s and early parts of this decade was a global trend.

3. *Central banks should consider adopting a broader definition of stability than pure price stability, based on a single basket of goods.* Of course, we want price stability, but we also want financial stability. This doesn't mean that central banks should target asset prices. But a central bank should maintain a sense of proportion. If the prices of consumer goods are stable while those of real estate and securities are sky-rocketing, these are instabilities a central bank should not ignore.

The Fed ignored the property bubble, on the spurious grounds that such bubbles are difficult to measure. This is complete nonsense. Given the near-linearity of house prices over long periods, anyone equipped with a pen and ruler can identify a house price bubble. It is really quite simple. You have a bubble when real house prices rise above your trend line by a sufficient amount for a sufficient time.

There was a debate among economists as to whether central banks should be in the business of pricking bubbles. This is an unfortunate metaphor. If you put it like this, of course, central banks should not prick bubbles. But they should take developments in the securities and real estate markets into account when assessing monetary stability. A central bank should also take monetary developments into account. I am not proposing a return to monetary targeting—in fact nobody is. But explicitly and proudly ignoring monetary developments, as the Fed has done, is also a mistake.

So these are my proposals. It is a smaller list than the one currently under discussion at the global level, but in some respects it is a far more ambitious list. You might say it is too ambitious—not realistic. Perhaps. But I warn you that our definition of what constitutes realism can change in a very short time. If someone had predicted a meltdown of the global financial system and the global economy two years ago, you would have called this person unrealistic.

And then it happened.

EPILOGUE: WHEN THE CRISIS IS OVER ...

This crisis, as with those that have preceded it, will eventually end. And if this crisis ends up being worse than predicted in this book, or if takes longer, then this more severe crisis will also end some time. As hard as it is to imagine now, in the spring of 2009, there will come a time when banks are no longer in trouble. What will the postcrisis age look like?

Free-market capitalism will survive, of course, but this statement is as true as it is meaningless. The quarter-century between the deregulation of U.S. financial markets in the 1980s and the outbreak of the financial crisis in August 2007 was the age of Anglo-Saxon, transaction-oriented capitalism. It was Anglo-Saxon because it was dominated largely by U.S. institutions, because the two main financial centers of this system were New York and London, and because this world communicated in the English language.

It was transaction-oriented, in the sense that nontangible services, such as credits, were turned into tradable securities.

The financing of corporate mergers and acquisitions is another important part of this system of transaction-oriented capitalism. The investment bank organized the entire transaction, and everything associated with it.

And it was capitalism, in its rawest form, almost a parody of capitalism, of the sort similar to that described by Karl Marx in the context of nineteenth-century industrial capitalism: It was brutal, self-seeking, and unsustainable. Since the days of Marx, industrial capitalism has changed out of recognition. It was necessary for the survival of the capitalist system. We will be witnessing a similar transformation, more than 100 years later, in financial capitalism.

So what will this mean? First of all, finance will shrink in size and in relative importance, and it will focus on different activities. Finance will still fulfill its main economic tasks of intermediation across distance and time, but to fulfill those functions, there is no need for finance to be as large as it is today. And society will also have to find a way to make finance work in its best interests, to use finance to help with real-world problems, such as the provision of social security systems.

Finance will have to compete much harder with other industries for the best people on the job market. The financial industry will no longer be able to take it for granted that it can recruit the best graduates from the best universities. There will be competition from industry, and even the newly strengthened public sector.

Talented young people will no longer necessarily want to become investment bankers, or hedge fund managers. These jobs were considered to be "cool" only a few years ago. This is no longer so. The standing of banks in our society has already declined, and bankers have already lost social status. We have heard stories that investment bankers no longer like to admit openly what kind of job they do out of sheer embarrassment. As the financial crisis turns into an extremely deep economic crisis, expect the public to extract more revenge on finance, and bankers in particular.

Salaries and bonuses will fall. Without a transaction-oriented shadow banking system, the ability to extract rents so easily, in the form of excessive salaries and bonus payments, will neither be justifiable nor achievable. Even without any further regulation, high bonuses will become unsustainable. And there will be further regulation. Of that there is no doubt.

Will globalization survive? Yes, but it will need to be much better managed. Imbalances as such are not bad things. But they, too, have to be managed. The world will also have to create new governance structures to manage the accompanying financial flows of globalization in a much more sustainable way. If not, imbalances will simply shrink, which is not necessarily good. It implies that much less money will chase through the global financial capitals. If we get this right, we will have found the way to make globalization socially more acceptable, and economically more sustainable. But this implies even harder times for global finance.

It is also very likely that the period following Anglo-Saxon transaction-oriented capitalism will see the emergence of a new multipolar order. The dominance of the dollar is an important element in the geostrategic supremacy of the United States. It gave the United States the exorbitant privilege to wage costly wars, to run up huge asset price bubbles, and set real interest rates at negative levels for long periods of time—and to do all that without experiencing the kind of total financial collapse Argentina suffered at the beginning of this decade. The United States was able to do all this because of its unique position at the hub of the global economy, and because of the role of the dollar as the world's largest reserve currency.

Those days will come to an end. The United States will remain an extremely dynamic economy, far more dynamic than Europe will ever be. But the Americans will have to come to terms with the new realities of multipolar economic power. The American people will realize that the dollar is not just their currency, and "someone else's problem," as a former U.S. Treasury Secretary once famously remarked. It will be their problem, too.

In this new world order, Asia will play a bigger role, and so, the author believes, will Europe. The latter is an unfashionable view nowadays. But I believe that over time, the euro will increase its importance as a global reserve and transaction currency at the expense of the dollar. It will not replace the dollar, but its weight will increase significantly. Over time, I would also expect the European financial markets to be more integrated, and to offer viable alternatives for Asian and Middle Eastern investors. In currency terms, the world will become bipolar. In industrial terms, however, the order will be multipolar. The center of gravity will no doubt be shifting toward Asia, but this process will probably take longer than some of the enthusiastic globalists think.

But the really good news is that the best talent of the next generation will no longer be devoted to moving wealth from one corner of the globe to another. There are more important things to do in the twenty-first century. Nobler tasks will emerge.

I would also hazard another prediction: We may lose our addiction to bubbles, at least for a while. Another bubble will come eventually. It always does as our brief history of global financial bubbles in the Appendix shows. But not for a while.

The twenty-first century will be able to finally begin.

APPENDIX: BUBBLES OF THE PAST

I'm forever blowing bubbles,
Pretty bubbles in the air.
They fly so high,
Nearly reach the sky,
Then like my dreams,
They fade and die.
Fortune's always hiding,
I've looked everywhere,
I'm forever blowing bubbles,
Pretty bubbles in the air.

—American folk song, 1919

Financial crises are nothing new. A number of historical comparisons have been made throughout the current crisis. They include, of course, comparisons with the Great

Depression, which was preceded by the 1929 stock market crash, and the Asian financial crisis of the 1990s. Although none of the past crises provide an exact parallel, they have all shared a number of features. In this sense, economic history offers a few enlightening insights.

Bubbles are among the most fascinating phenomena of financial markets. They have existed for as long as financial markets have been around. In fact, they are even older. To understand our crisis, it is important to take a look at how and why bubbles develop.

Financial markets live on expectations, because the value of an investment is determined by events in the future. Investors in the commodities markets speculate in the summer on how the wheat harvest will turn out in the fall. The value of a share is computed, at least in theory, as the discounted value of a company's expected future profits, divided by the number of shares. Financial theory is based on the assumption that the totality of investors behaves rationally. This doesn't mean that everyone always makes the right decisions, but merely that the majority of investors do not allow themselves to be misled all of the time. In other words, people learn from their mistakes. The assumption of rationality makes it easy to construct economic and financial models. A single bubble would not defy that assumption, but the regular recurrence of bubbles is not consistent with the assumption of rationality.

We know, of course, that people are capable of irrational behavior, even for prolonged periods of time. A financial market bubble is an example of the irrational behavior of a large majority of investors. During the bubble, everyone is convinced that their behavior is rational. Only in retrospect do people realize how irrational they have been.

The late John Kenneth Galbraith wrote a wonderful book about this topic, titled *A Short History of Financial Euphoria*. He described that bubbles have several characteristics in common. The first is infectious euphoria. People who normally do not invest allow themselves to come under the spell of the bubble. The second phenomenon is the attempt to rationalize extremely high prices with spurious arguments, such as the dot-com theories that arose around 2000, or even more abstruse theories. The pseudo-theory on which the credit boom was based was the assumption that mathematical innovations in the financial sectors led to a more efficient allocation of loans. Loans were made to people and companies that would not have qualified as borrowers in the past. Lending to people who cannot possibly repay is not exactly new, but the interesting thing is that there is always some new element in the story that makes it appear to be true—at least to a majority of people.

The third characteristic of a bubble is a sharp and sudden overall rise in lending. In addition to speculating with their own money, investors borrow money to finance their speculation. The same applies to the credit market itself, where not only securities are based on loans but where speculation is also financed with borrowed funds. It goes without saying that this sort of arrangement can quickly turn into a vicious circle.

Galbraith made a remarkable and highly controversial observation in this regard, and in doing so he hit upon the philosophical core of the problem. The question is whether something like innovation is even possible in financial markets. Galbraith wrote:

> *As to new financial instruments, experience establishes a firm rule ... that financial operations do not lend themselves to innovation. What is recurrently so described and celebrated is, without exception, a small variation on an established design, one that owes its distinctive character to the aforementioned brevity of the financial memory. The world of finance hails the invention of the wheel over and over again, often in a slightly more unstable version. All financial innovation involves, in one form or another, the creation of debt secured in greater or lesser adequacy by real assets. . . . All crises have involved debt that, in one fashion or another, has become dangerously out of scale in relation to the underlying means of payment.*

To put it crudely, what makes a bubble a bubble is not the fact that grandmother closes her savings account to buy stocks, but that she closes the savings account, borrows five times as much as she has saved and, using her savings and borrowed funds, buys a highly risky tranche of a complex derivative, one that she doesn't understand and with which she is providing a hedge fund with the guarantee of the creditworthiness of a junk bond.

The prerequisite for any bubble is, of course, the existence of a market, although it does not necessarily have to be a financial market. One of the oddest bubbles of all was the Dutch tulip bubble in the seventeenth century, which had many traits of modern bubbles. For many people, the notion that a financial bubble could be created with stocks and other securities borders on the miraculous. But that a tulip bulb could be responsible for a bubble never ceases to amaze even experts on economic history.

The Tulip Bubble

Although most people nowadays see the tulip as a typical Dutch product, it was unknown in the Netherlands until well into the sixteenth century. Galbraith wrote that tulip bulbs were brought to Amsterdam in the mid-sixteenth century on ships from Constantinople. The tulip quickly achieved a status of prosperity and cultivated life.

But in the early seventeenth century, the tulip also became an object of speculation in the Netherlands. The entire country was caught up in the speculation, and many people became rich.

Galbraith wrote that in 1636 a single tulip bulb cost as much as a carriage and two horses. But this was only the beginning of the bubble. Charles Mackay wrote in his 1841 book, *Extraordinary Popular Delusions and the Madness of Crowds*, one of the most important reference works on this episode:

> *The demand for tulips of a rare species increased so much in the year 1636, that regular marts for their sale were established on the Stock Exchange of Amsterdam,*

in Rotterdam, Harlaem, Leyden, Alkmar, Hoorn, and other towns. Symptoms of gambling now became, for the first time, apparent. The stock-jobbers, ever on the alert for a new speculation, dealt largely in tulips, making use of all the means they so well knew how to employ, to cause fluctuations in prices. At first, as in all these gambling mania, confidence was at its height, and every body gained. The tulip-jobbers speculated in the rise and fall of the tulip stocks, and made large profits by buying when prices fell, and selling out when they rose. Many individuals grew suddenly rich. A golden bait hung temptingly out before the people, and one after the other, they rushed to the tulip-marts, like flies around a honey-pot. Every one imagined that the passion for tulips would last forever, and that the wealthy from every part of the world would send to Holland, and pay whatever prices were asked for them. The riches of Europe would be concentrated on the shores of the Zuyder Zee, and poverty banished from the favoured clime of Holland. Nobles, citizens, farmers, mechanics, sea-men, footmen, maid-servants, even chimney-sweeps and old clothes-women, dabbled in tulips. People of all grades converted their property into cash, and invested it in flowers. Houses and lands were offered for sale at ruinously low prices, or assigned in payment of bargains made at the tulip-mart. Foreigners became smitten with the same frenzy, and money poured into Holland from all directions. The prices of the necessaries of life rose again by degrees: houses and lands, horses and carriages, and luxuries of every sort, rose in value with them, and

*for some months Holland seemed the very antecham-
ber of Plutus. The operations of the trade became so
extensive and so intricate, that it was found necessary to draw up a code of laws for the guidance of
the dealers. Notaries and clerks were also appointed,
who devoted themselves exclusively to the interests of
the trade. The designation of public notary was hardly
known in some towns, that of tulip-notary usurping
its place. In the smaller towns, where there was no
exchange, the principal tavern was usually selected as
the "show-place," where high and low traded in tulips,
and confirmed their bargains over sumptuous enter-
tainments. These dinners were sometimes attended by
two or three hundred persons, and large vases of tulips,
in full bloom, were placed at regular intervals upon
the tables and sideboards for their gratification during
the repast.*

The tulip mania ended in 1637. No one is quite sure what
triggered the beginning of the end. For unknown reasons, a few
well-known speculators suddenly sold their tulips and pulled
out of the market. Their withdrawal triggered a mass panic.
Many speculators had borrowed money to buy tulips, hoping
that they would increase in value, which would allow them to
repay their loans and make a profit. Rich noblemen became
paupers overnight. In fact, the entire country fell into poverty
and suffered a deep depression that lasted for many years. The
blame game started instantly.

In his comment on this and other bubbles, Galbraith
observed that human memory is short. Whenever a bubble has

burst, the financial sector initially becomes immune to euphoria. For several years, the possibility of rising prices was viewed with great skepticism. Galbraith wrote, in this regard: "For practical purposes, the financial memory should be assumed to last, at a maximum, no more than 20 years."

The tulip bubble is probably one of the most unusual phenomena in economic history. Although the financial markets were not nearly as developed then as they are today, there are several surprising parallels nonetheless. As irrational as the tulip bubble may appear from today's perspective, the rapidly rising value of tulip bulbs seemed rational to people at the time. Even professionals were caught up in the tulip mania, just as there are victims of the current credit crisis who are not exactly widows and orphans, but hardened bankers who made the mistake of believing in their own lies.

Galbraith was completely correct in one respect. When it comes to bubbles, history repeats itself almost perfectly. Euphoria inevitably develops, and with it comes the willingness to take irrational risks.

The Panic of 1907

Another bubble, the panic of 1907, also shares a few structural characteristics with the current situation. As with today's situation, the panic of 1907 developed in the banking system itself. It began with an attempt by one speculator to manipulate the market for copper. This led to a chain of events that almost resulted in the complete collapse of the American banking system. For those who wish to understand today's problems, the crash of 1907 offers several important lessons.

Around 1900, American banks were permitted to accept the public's savings, but they could not manage assets. This task was performed by trust companies, which, in a sense, were the precursors of the modern-day hedge funds. Like today, there were gaps in an otherwise strict regulatory system at the time. Although banks were not permitted to perform the functions of a trust, they could own trusts. Bank directors could work for trusts, and vice versa, so that the separation between the two entities merely existed on paper. As strict as the regulations were, bankers always knew how best to circumvent the rules.

One difference between then and now is that there was no central bank at the time. Instead, there was an entity called the Clearing House Association, which was under the control of the banks but did not include the trust companies. The Clearing House was responsible for honoring the banks' checks and ensuring liquidity in the market. In other words, it functioned as a financier of last resort. It also performed a regulatory function, and it was considered a great honor at the time to be appointed to the board of the Clearing House Association. This was the underlying situation.

The crash began with a speculation that had gone wrong in October 1907. F. Augustus Heinze, a well-known speculator in the copper business, employed a bold speculative strategy—mercilessly buying up the shares of United Copper—in an attempt to drive up the price of the metal. But his speculation failed. Heinze lost $50 million, an unimaginable amount of money at the time, and his loss had a negative effect on the markets. If Heinze had merely been a copper speculator, his speculation would not have led to a financial market crisis. However, he was also a banker, but one who even admitted that he knew little about the banking business. Heinze owned a provincial bank, but he was also the president of the Mercantile National Bank, a position from which he resigned immediately after his losses in the copper industry became public.

Nevertheless, his resignation did not prevent a run on the Mercantile National Bank the next day, because depositors feared, erroneously, that the bank had something to do with Heinze's business. Unlike today, savings deposits were not insured at the time, and so-called bank runs were a relatively common occurrence in the nineteenth and early twentieth centuries. The bank run on the Mercantile National Bank was promptly stopped when the Clearing House Association stepped in. It was believed, and even reported in the newspapers, that the move had brought an end to the crisis. But this was a false assumption. Things were about to get much worse.

Another run occurred at the same time, on the Knickerbocker Trust Company—not a bank but, as the name reveals, a trust. Knickerbocker's president, Charles T. Barney, was a close associate of Heinze, and Heinze's negative aura was responsible for the run on Knickerbocker. The crisis came to a dramatic head with Barney's suicide, which in turn led to Knickerbocker's investors withdrawing $8 million within three hours the next morning. Knickerbocker closed its doors to the public the next day.

The banking crisis spread like wildfire after that. Investors withdrew their money from the banking system, and the banks, too, lost confidence in one another and stopped lending each other money. The panic of 1907 was certainly not the worst economic crisis in U.S. history—that distinction still goes to the 1929 crash—but the dramatic structure of the earlier crisis is a prime example of how seemingly inconsequential factors—faulty speculation in this case—can bring down an already ailing banking system.

The 1907 crisis did not end until a few days later. At first, J.P. Morgan, the most legendary American banker of all time, who was 70 at the time, intervened and pledged large sums of money to shore up the banking system. In the end, Morgan decided not to rescue Knickerbocker but another trust, the Trust Company of America.

The government intervened and sent then-Treasury Secretary George B. Cortelyou to New York to pledge government assistance. The legendary tycoon John D. Rockefeller also provided financial support for the banks, and within a few days the panic gradually subsided. On October 24, 1907, the Trust Company survived a run, heralding the end of the panic. Morgan bolstered the New York Stock Exchange, which was also on the verge of collapse, and a measure of calm returned to Wall Street in the ensuing days.

According to Stephen Quinn, an economics professor at the University of Texas at Arlington-Fort Worth, there are a number of parallels between the 1907 bank panic and the current situation.

First, there are significant similarities between trusts and hedge funds. Both forms of organization exist for the purpose of circumventing strict regulation.

Second, when the panic erupted, no one knew exactly where the risks were. The available information was asymmetrical.

Third, the trusts, which were not organized in the Clearing House system, faced difficulties during the panic similar to those faced by today's hedge funds or bank-owned investment firms, which are also not subject to Federal Reserve supervision.

And finally, the 1907 crisis led to a flood of completely new banking regulations. First, there was the Aldrich-Vreeland Act, which provided a new regulatory structure for the emergency financing of banks. After that, the Federal Reserve System was created and the Clearing House system was abolished. As a result, a clear division was drawn between the banks themselves and the bank reserve system, hence the name Federal Reserve.

The purpose of this appendix is not to present a proper history of financial bubbles, but merely to provide a few highlights. Our crisis naturally also contains elements from the Great Depression and Japan's lost decade in the 1990s.

The most important similarity with the Great Depression is the speed of global contagion. Between 1929 and 1932 global trade volumes declined by a total of 25 to 35 percent. If you look at the value of global trade, the decline looks even more dramatic, but this is due to deflation, which lowers the prices of merchandise goods.

In the three-month period between November 2008 and January 2009 global trade fell by a total of 20 percent. If you annualized this number, you get to a rate of 60 percent. The reader will know whether this trend continued by the fall of

2009. It probably did not. But even with 20 percent we were well on the way to a depression-era fall in global trade.

The United States was the epicenter of this crisis, but the countries worst affected were the classic exporters, Japan and Germany in particular. These two countries normally run extremely large trade surpluses, and their economies have become dependent on global trade.

Why would trade fall by so much? There are several explanations. The engine of global economic growth, the persistent imbalances inherent in the Bretton Woods II machinery, essentially collapsed, as the U.S. consumer ceased to be the buyer of last resort. I expect this situation to last for some time, as U.S. households adjust their balance sheets. Exports of finished goods to the United States subsequently collapsed, and so did the production of those goods in Asia, and that in turn affected the intra-Asian trade in intermediate goods and raw materials.

The financial crisis also had a direct impact on trade finance, which was in some cases not available as banks mistrusted each other's ability to make good on their promises—a trust on which trade finance depends. And the financial crisis also resulted in tighter credit standards worldwide, so that companies faced difficulties to obtain credit for investment, and consumers faced tighter standards for credits. By the spring of 2009, we certainly did not understand all the mechanisms of the downturn, but the financial crisis gave rise to a severe recession, which in turn exacerbated the financial crisis, resulting in a vicious circle.

The problem during the Great Depression was exacerbated by the gold standard, which acted as a main shock transmission mechanism. This was not a problem in the current situation. In fact, there are many significant differences between the two crises, both in terms of the nature of the crisis, and the policy response. But the crises have in common that each country understood the crisis as a principally domestic affair, rather than as a problem they have to solve jointly. The lack of effective international coordination in both cases prolonged and deepened the crises.

The Japanese experience also holds important policy lessons. There are obvious superficial parallels in that both the Japanese and our crises were preceded by property bubbles, which turned into complete banking crises as banks held toxic assets on their balance sheets. In Japan, the authorities initially reacted with a delayed macroeconomic response, but interest rates did eventually fall to zero, and fiscal policy did expand, yet the country was not able to secure a recovery as economic growth stagnated.

During its lost decade Japan failed to solve its main structural problem, a banking sector laden with toxic assets, a problem successive governments failed to tackle until the early years of the new millennium. The Japanese government finally ended the financial crisis by forcing banks to write down the bad assets and to accept government money in the form of new equity capital. Herein lies an important lesson for our crisis.

The Japanese experience taught us that a macroeconomic policy response may be necessary but it is clearly not sufficient to solve an economic slump with a deep banking crisis. You need to fix the banks, and this means, you need to find a mechanism to help the banks write down the bad assets, and provide for new capital. In the case of our crisis, the task is infinitely more difficult, because the banking sector itself had become bloated during the bubble. We need not only to recapitalize the banks but at the same time also shrink the banking sector, but at a much larger proportional and absolute degree than was the case in Japan. The Geithner and Summers plan announced in March 2009 was at best a partial answer to the first problem but provided no answer to the second. The European bank recapitalization plans, consisting mostly of voluntary recapitalization programs, did not solve the problem either.

We seem to be repeating some of the mistakes committed during the Great Depression, and those occurring 60 years later in Japan.

GLOSSARY AND LIST OF ABBREVIATIONS

F or ease of reference, a glossary and list of abbreviations of the most important terms in the text are provided below. Words in *italics* have separate entries.

AAA or Aaa—The highest rating awarded by a rating agency for a fixed interest security.

ABCP—See *asset-backed commercial paper.*

ABS—See *asset-backed security*.

Asset-backed commercial paper—Money market securities that are backed by assets. In the ABCP market, *SIVs*, for example, borrow money on a short-term basis and deposit loans as collateral.

Asset-backed security—A *bond* backed by a group of real assets as collateral.

Bank for International Settlements (BIS)—Often called the central bank of central banks. Plays an important role in international cooperation among central banks and a very important role in the formation of international capital regulations. The *Basle I* and *Basle II* rules were named after the Swiss city where the BIS has its headquarters.

Basle I—A 1988 accord that prescribes capital adequacy rules. Under these rules, the loans issued by banks are subject to limits that depend on a specific measure of the bank's core capital—the so-called tier 1 capital. To calculate whether a bank fulfills the capital adequacy requirements, loans are risk-weighted. Certain types of credit, such as business loans, are categorized as risky, while others, such as loans to other banks, are categorized as less risky.

Basle II—A successor accord to *Basle I*, which came into effect in Europe in 2008. Basle II reforms the *Basel I* accord in various ways, one of which is that the credit/equity capital quota is no longer computed on the basis of rigid rules, but on the basis of credit ratings prepared by the bank.

BBA—British Bankers Association.

BIS—See *Bank for International Settlements*.

Bond—A fixed-interest security that usually pays a coupon (similar to an interest rate). At the end of the term, or maturity, the face value of the bond is repaid. There are various forms of bonds, such as the *zero-coupon bond*.

Call—A call option is a financial derivative security that gives its holder the right, but not the obligation, to buy an underlying security at a given price, the so-called strike price. Call options are used to hedge, or to speculate on rising security prices. The opposite of a call is a *put*.

Carry trade—A short-term trading strategy that consists, for example, of borrowing money in a country with low interest rates and then investing it in a country with higher rates. A typical carry trade consisted in borrowing money in Japanese yen, investing the money overnight in Europe or the United States, where money market interest rates were higher than in Japan, and repaying the loan the next day.

CD—Certificate of Deposit.

CDO—See *collateralized debt obligation*.

CDS—See *credit default swap*.

Collateralized debt obligation—A credit market security, which bundles pools of loans and transforms them into securities of various grades. There are various types of CDOs, including those with the sole purpose of providing regulatory relief under the Basle capital adequacy requirements (balance sheet CDO), and those that are actively managed. The latter are similar to investment trusts. Many CDOs invested only in *mortgage-backed securities*, while others invested in other assets, such as credit card debt or car loans.

CMO—See *collateralized mortgage obligation*.

Commercial paper—Money market securities with terms of up to two years. Usually issued by banks or large companies for short-term financing.

Conduit—A special purpose vehicle established by banks, with the purpose of engaging in credit market transactions. In many cases, conduits assume the bank's loans and transform them into *tranches* of securities. A conduit is managed directly by a bank.

Copula—A term in statistics. A copula is a common distribution of a number of random variables, the individual components of which are uniformly distributed on a uniform interval.

Correlation—A term from statistics. Two time series are correlated when there is a (usually) linear relationship between the movements of one of the series and those of the other, such as securities prices, either concurrently or within a fixed interval. For example, there is a correlation between the price of gold and future inflation expectations. However, a correlation that can be measured statistically says nothing about causality.

Covenant—An agreement attached to a loan, either in written or verbal form. Many important but subordinate aspects of a credit agreement, such as disclosure requirements, are regulated in the covenant.

Cov-light—Credit agreements in which the terms normally regulated in the *covenant* are relaxed for the benefit of the borrower.

CP—commercial paper.

Credit default swap—A financial instrument in the credit market used as insurance against default. The buyer of a CDS is the one who obtains the insurance. As a rule, the buyer pays a quarterly premium to the seller. In the event of a default, the seller must compensate the buyer. The reference value is a *bond*, or a basket of bonds, usually in the order of $10 million. A CDS is quoted in basis points. A quotation of 200 basis points means that $200,000 is payable as the premium.

Credit market—A part of the financial market in which securities are traded, which are based on loans, such as *MBS*s, *ABS*s, and *CDO*s.

Credit spread—The difference between the interest rate for a security and the interest rate for a safe government bond, such as a U.S. Treasury bond. If the credit spread is small, as was the case during the bubble, investors are especially risk-friendly, and they accept a low risk premium for the purchase of a security. One of the characteristics of the August 2007 crisis was a sudden rise in the credit spread.

ECB—European Central Bank.

Equity—The riskiest *tranche* of a CDO, also known as a junior tranche. Equity *tranches* are usually not rated by the *rating agencies*. The term "equity" normally refers to stocks, but in this case we are not talking about stocks but *bonds*. The only reason this *tranche* is called equity is that it carries similar risks.

Euribor—Euro Interbank Offered Rate, a daily reference rate in the interbank business for banks operating in the Euro area.

Fannie Mae—Federal National Mortgage Association.

Freddie Mac—Federal Home Loan Mortgage Corporation.

FT—*Financial Times*.

Hedge—A safeguard against risk. Hedging instruments include options, which allow, but do not oblige, an investor to buy securities at a predetermined price on a specific date in the future.

Hedge fund—An investment fund that is overseen by regulators to hedge investments using methods such as short selling and trading in options.

IMF—International Monetary Fund.

Interbank market—A *money market* in which banks lend and borrow money for short periods and without collateral. Interest rates in money markets, such as *LIBOR* or *EURIBOR*, are generally close to the central banks' prime or base rates. These interest rates rose significantly during the credit crisis in August 2007, and have remained elevated for most of the crisis.

ISDA—International Swap and Derivatives Association.

Junior—See *tranche*.

Leveraged loan—A loan for a specific project, such as a takeover, in which the bank puts up most of the finance. A leveraged loan is riskier and carries higher interest rates.

LIBOR—London Interbank Offered Rate, one of the most important interest rates in the *money market*.

Long—Investors are long a security when they buy and hold that security. Investors are long if they expect the security to appreciate in the future. Most private investors are long.

LTCM—Long-Term Capital Management, a hedge fund that ran into serious financial difficulties in 1998, bringing Wall Street to the brink of a systematic crisis.

Mark-to-market—An accounting term. The book value of a security is calculated on the basis of current market prices. Stocks, government bonds, and currency are all mark-to-market.

Mark-to-model—A term signifying that the price of a security is calculated using a mathematical model, but not on the basis of market prices. The *tranches* of a CDO are generally mark-to-model, because CDOs are not traded in liquid markets. The problem with the mark-to-model strategy is that in times of liquidity bottlenecks, the models yield higher prices than can be achieved in the markets.

MBS—See *mortgage-backed security*.

Mezzanine—The intermediate *tranche* of a CDO.

Money market—A market for money, in which securities are issued with terms of up to two years. A distinction is made between the *interbank market* and the *commercial paper* market.

Monolines—Highly specialized insurance companies whose business consisted of guaranteeing regular coupon payments of *bonds*. Monolines suffered heavy losses during the credit crisis.

Mortgage-backed security—A security with various *tranches*, backed by a mortgage.

Over-the-counter (OTC) market—A market in securities that involves direct, bank-to-bank transactions. In an OTC transaction, each buyer must find a seller. In other words, there is no exchange in which dealers agree to sell a security at a specific price. The credit market is almost exclusively an OTC market.

Prime broker—Generally a division of an investment bank that offers a full range of services for *hedge funds*.

Private equity groups—Financial companies that provide financing primarily for the restructuring of medium-sized companies, or for corporate takeovers.

Put—An option that gives the holder the right, but not the obligation, to sell an underlying security at a specified price, the strike price. A put option can be used to speculate on the decline of an underlying security price. A put is the opposite of a *call*. The Greenspan put mentioned in the text refers to a situation in which the U.S. central bank, the *Federal Reserve*, comes to the aid of speculators when the wider market faces a decline. In other words, speculators do not have to hedge against a fall in the overall market, because the central bank assumes that task.

Rating agencies—Private companies whose business is to rate securities, or *tranches* of securities. The three most important rating agencies are Moody's, Standard & Poor's, and Fitch.

Repo—Repurchase agreement, or securities repurchase agreement. A repo is a regular auction that a central bank uses to provide short-term capital to banks. The repo rate—the central bank's base or prime rate—is the interest rate for this type of loan. In technical terms, a repo is used by a central bank to purchase securities from banks for a specified period. At the end of that period, the central bank resells the securities to the banks at prices discounted by the repo rate.

S&P—Standard & Poor's.

Securitization—The conversion of nonloans into marketable securities.

Senior—The most secure *tranche* of a CDO, generally provided with a solid rating by the *rating agencies*.

Short—Investors are short a security by selling securities that they do not own (i.e., which they have to buy later). Investors are short when they are betting on a decline in the price of a security.

SIV—See *special investment vehicle*.

SIV-light—A *special investment vehicle* that obtains finance through the *ABCP* market.

Special investment vehicle—A company similar to a *conduit*, with the difference being that an SIV is not managed by a bank but by a third party.

Special purpose vehicle—Companies that are established to achieve certain objectives. These companies are generally not consolidated on the balance sheets of the companies or banks that have set them up.

SPV—See *special purpose vehicle*.

Subprime—Loans or mortgages issued to customers with a poor credit history. Before the crisis, subprime mortgages were often approved without verifying the income of the applicant. The credit crisis was triggered by a rise in defaults on subprime mortgages.

Swap—A financial instrument in which two parties agree to exchange cash flows. An important example is the interest rate swap, in which two parties exchange flows of variable and fixed interest payments. One party pays the second party the variable rate, generally *LIBOR* or *EURIBOR*, while the second party pays the fixed rate, known as the swap rate.

Syndicated loan—Generally a large loan granted to a borrower by several banks, with one bank playing a coordinating role.

Synthetic CDO—In the case of a normal CDO, credit serves as the collateral of the securities *tranches*. In a synthetic CDO, CDSs assume this role. Writing, i.e., selling, a CDS is in some respects similar to holding loans (i.e., you are entitled to a regular cash flow of payments).

Tranche—The French word for "slice." A tranche of an *asset-backed security* or CDO is a security with a (not always) clearly defined risk profile and a return that supposedly corresponds to the risk. There are several types of tranches. A *senior* tranche, or senior debt, refers to the tranche with the lowest risk and lowest return. A *senior* tranche typically has good or very good credit ratings. The *junior*, or *equity*, tranche carries the highest risk and offers the highest potential return. Between the two, there is the *mezzanine* tranche, also referred to as interim financing.

Value at risk—A statistical method used by banks and investment companies to calculate their risk. The method has been exposed as faulty.

VaR—See *value at risk*.

Zero-coupon bond—A *bond* that pays no coupons and which, in return, is purchased at a discount from its face value. The reason for this type of structure often lies in a country's tax system, in which income (coupons) are taxed differently than capital gains.

RESOURCES

About Bubbles

The classic short text about bubbles: John Kenneth Galbraith, *A Short History of Financial Euphoria*, Penguin Books, 1990.

The best reference on the tulip bubble: Charles Mackay, *Memoirs of Extraordinary Popular Delusions and the Madness of Crowds*, London: Richard Bentley, 1841.

My two favorite references on the Great Depression: Charles Kindleberger, *The World in Depression 1929–1939*, University of California Press, 1986, and Barry Eichengreen, *Golden Fetters: The Gold Standard and the Great Depression, 1919–1939*, Oxford University Press, 1992.

The best reference on Japan: Adam Posen, *Restoring Japan's Economic Growth, Peterson Institute for International Economics*, 1998.

About Modern Finance

If you are interested in learning about modern financial markets, the following is a list of excellent selections. Das is a good narrative. Cecchetti is an excellent textbook. Maxey is a brilliant analysis of how the short-long games in the credit market worked. Fabozzi and colleagues tell us how to construct a toxic financial instrument in our living room.

Satjayit Das, *Traders, Guns and Money: Knowns and Unknowns in the Dazzling World of Derivatives*, Prentice Hall, 2006.

Stephen G. Cecchetti, *Money, Banking, and Financial Markets*, McGraw-Hill International Edition, 2007.

Henry Maxey, "Cracking the Credit Market Code," Study for the Centre of Financial Innovation, London, May 2007.

Frank J. Fabozzi, Henry A. Davis, and Moorad Choudhry, *Introduction to Structured Finance*, Wiley Finance, 2006.

About the Mathematics

The following are books and articles on mathematical finance. Nielsen is a great introduction into the mathematics of finance with a good balance of rigor and intuition; Schönbucher does the hard math on credit derivatives; Taleb presents a criticism; as does Mikosch.

Lars Tyge Nielsen, *Pricing and Hedging of Derivative Securities*, Oxford University Press, 1999.

Philipp J. Schönbucher, *Credit Derivatives Pricing Models: Models, Pricing and Implementation*, Wiley, 2003.
Nassim Nicholas Taleb, *Fooled by Randomness, The Hidden Role of Chance in Life and in the Markets*, Random House, 2005.
Thomas Mikosch, "Copulas, Tales and Facts," Working Paper, November 2005, discussion paper initiated at the 4th International Conference on Extreme Value Analysis in Gothenburg, Sweden.

About Bretton Woods II and Global Imbalances

Dooley and colleagues provide the classic text on BWII. Wolf presents a trenchant analysis of finance and global imbalances; Eichengreen is the book to read on global capital flows.

Michael P. Dooley, David Folkerts-Landau, and Peter Garber, "An Essay on the Revived Bretton Woods System," Nber Working Paper 9971, http://www.nber.org/papers/w9971.
Martin Wolf, *Fixing Global Finance*, Johns Hopkins University Press, 2008.
Barry Eichengreen, *Global Imbalances and the Lessons of Bretton Woods*, MIT Press, 2006.

INDEX

Note: Boldface numbers indicate illustrations.

CPSIA information can be obtained
at www.ICGtesting.com
Printed in the USA
BVHW010845180821
614477BV00013B/2